"Patrick Kelly runs his business like he lives his straightforward, trusting, and with tremendous zes in both arenas speaks to the power of his approach
—*Joseph Neubauer, Chair*
ARAMA

"I thoroughly enjoyed reading *Faster Company*. . . extraordinary example of entrepreneurial spirit focus on respect for the dignity of people and true to customer service and loyalty."
—*Carlos Cantu, Presi*
ServiceM

"As you read this book, you'll find yourself checki *ster's Collegiate Dictionary* to see if there's a pictu Kelly next to the word maverick. . . . What I like b book personally is that it fosters the idea of 'givi sharing the wealth. Read this book and you'll lo changes the way you run your business!"   –

"What makes Pat Kelly a rare billion-dollar busin that he is also a great teacher. . . . It's why we' invited Pat to spend time teaching his lessons to the world's emerging growth businesses. Nobody d
—*Verne Harnish, founder, Young Entrepreneu*
and founder, Master of Bus

"A company is only as good as its people, and Pat how to motivate people. He shares his motivati and other creative business strategies in this fa straightforward book. He tells it like it is!"
—*Jim Moran, automotive entrepreneur*
and founder, JM Family H

FASTER
COMPANY

FASTER
COMPANY

Building the World's Nuttiest, Turn-on-a-Dime, Home-Grown, Billion-Dollar Business

---

PATRICK KELLY
WITH JOHN CASE

John Wiley & Sons, Inc.

NEW YORK • CHICHESTER • BRISBANE • WEINHEIM • SINGAPORE • TORONTO

Published by John Wiley & Sons, Inc.
Published simultaneously in Canada.

This publication is designed to provide accurate and authoritative information in regard to the subject matter covered. It is sold with the understanding that the publisher is not engaged in rendering professional services. If professional advice or other expert assistance is required, the services of a competent professional person should be sought.

Library of Congress Cataloging-in-Publication Data:

Kelly, Patrick, 1947–
    Faster company : building the world's nuttiest, turn-on-a-dime, home-grown, billion-dollar business / by Patrick Kelly with John Case.
      p.   cm.
    Includes index.
    ISBN 0-471-24211-X (cloth : alk. paper)
    1. New business enterprises—United States. 2. Small business—United States. 3. Success in business—United States. I. Case.
John, 1944–   . II. Title.
HD62.5.K44 1998
658.02'2—dc21   97-45080
                                                    CIP

Printed in the United States of America.

10 9 8 7 6 5 4 3 2 1

This book is dedicated to the thousands of boys who have lived at the Virginia Home for Boys, and the thousands more who will. One of the oldest orphanages in America, the Virginia Home for Boys gave me the tools to succeed in life.

Teamwork, sharing, getting along with others, and trust were the values I learned at the Home. Today I endeavor to get PSSers—our employees—to share these values with their fellow employees.

—And they do!!!

CONTENTS

FOREWORD

Dave Thomas

**Founder and Senior Chairman,
Wendy's International**

There are three things I like about this book and that I think you will, too.

The first is that it shows how Pat Kelly built a truly amazing business.

PSS/World Medical isn't in any kind of glamorous, high-tech industry. But it has grown to a billion dollars in annual revenues in only 15 years just by taking care of its customers and giving them a level of service they can't get anywhere else. There are a whole bunch of lessons in the book about how to lead a company that can achieve that kind of success. If you take these lessons to heart, you'll be a better businessperson.

The second thing I like is that Pat doesn't fall into the trap so many others fall into. He doesn't believe that there's a contradiction between *people* and *profits*.

While so many businesses have been downsizing, PSS has been creating jobs. While the gap between rich and poor has been growing, PSS has been making millionaires out of truck drivers and accountants. Pat's company is not only phenomenally successful, it's also a great place to work. You'll learn from this book how to create a company where people work hard and play hard—and have a darn good time in the process.

Third, Pat Kelly is a man with a mission.

Like me, he had a difficult childhood. He spent most of his early years in the Virginia Home for Boys, in Richmond. Today, Pat's business is tremendously important to him—but what's even more important are the boys and girls who don't have a family that can take care of them. Pat has set up a foundation to provide support for the Home and others like it. He and his brother guarantee a college education to any boy from the Virginia Home who graduates from high school. All his proceeds from this book will be donated to the foundation. But Pat is the kind of guy who gives more than money. If you visit him at his home in Florida, for instance, you might be sharing the guest quarters with a couple of kids from the Home who are down for the weekend. Pat hangs out with them and shows them a good time. But what he's really teaching them is that they, too, can achieve their dreams.

That's a lesson we all need to learn. Who knows? Maybe this book can help you achieve yours.

PREFACE

Suppose I told you that you could build a company that could grow at close to 60 percent a year every year for 15 years. Your company wouldn't be in high tech or, indeed, in any kind of glitzy industry. It could be in a mundane, everyday business. It would gobble up market share the old-fashioned way, which is to say, by shoving the competition out of the way. It would not only grow like gangbusters, it would also make a ton of money for its shareholders.

And suppose I added that your company would be considered a terrific place to work. It would be a place jobseekers would swarm to and that would hardly ever lose its best people to the competition. People would say they actually had fun working there. They'd also know they had a chance of making some serious money—in many cases, money beyond their wildest dreams.

Finally, suppose I said that this company would run with no policy manual. That the employees could fire their bosses. That truck drivers would have CEO on their business cards. That leaders—there are no "managers" at this company—would be required to study Plato and Dostoevsky. That big divisions of the business would be run by people still in their twenties.

Well, if you bumped into me on an airplane and I said all this to you, you'd probably figure I should have my head examined. Or that I was one of the bigger vendors of horse manure that you had run into in a while.

The fact is, though, all that stuff is exactly what I am about to say to you in this book. And if you read the book, you'll see that it isn't horse manure at all. It happened. We did it, at the company you'll learn about in the chapters that follow. What's more, there was no magic involved, just a willingness to do things differently from the way everybody else does them. No reason that you can't do things that way, too.

Of course, you'll want to read this book quickly. Because you really wouldn't want your competitors to get their hands on it first.

INTRODUCTION

The Meaning of Speed

This book is about how to build a particular kind of business—one that can do things its competitors can't do. But I didn't call it *Better Company* or *More Skillful Company*, I called it *Faster Company*. There's a reason for this.

Nobody creates a company in a vacuum. People build companies at particular times in history, in particular marketplaces. Henry Ford did a great job creating a business that could dominate the automobile marketplace of the early twentieth century. Theodore Vail, the man responsible for building AT&T into the powerhouse it became, had a vision of a single phone company spanning the United States and was able to translate that vision into reality. But times change. Technology changes, markets change, and tastes change. New businesses appear. Today, Ford Motor Co. is just one auto maker among many. AT&T is still a great enterprise—but it's beset on all sides by fierce and imaginative competitors who are, in some ways, better attuned to today's marketplace.

The hallmark of this marketplace, we know, is that nothing stands still. Products have short life cycles. Consumers are fickle. Competition is brutal, which means that no company can rest on its laurels. If it can't deliver a better product or service than it did last year, it might as well close up shop, because it isn't going to be around long.

What kind of company can thrive in this marketplace? Well, a *fast* company, sure. Speed has become an icon of our era. UPS's slogan for a while was "Moving at the Speed of Business." Computer companies live and die on how quickly they can bring out a new model. The latest business magazine is actually called *Fast Company*. Trouble is, you could ask 15 people to define what a fast company is and you'd get 15 different responses. And a lot of those responses point you in exactly the wrong direction.

One idea, for example, is that a fast company has to be on the cutting edge of technology. It has to be in microchips, in software, in telecommunications, or in biotech.

If you believe this, I urge you to take a look at *Inc.* magazine's annual listings of the fastest-growing small companies. You'll find that plenty of these high-growth stars are in high-tech businesses, to be sure. But you'll also find many, many very successful businesses in such industries as parts manufacturing, payroll services, and catalog retailing. These aren't exactly glamorous niches— but somehow the businesses that make these lists are able to grow and prosper. The company I helped start, PSS/World Medical, sells such fancy high-tech products as Band-Aids, toilet paper, and syringes. Yet we grew from startup—zero revenues—to revenues of more than a billion dollars in only 15 years. Evidently there's something about the way we do business that fits today's marketplace.

A second definition of *fast company* is an organization that wheels and deals. You know the type, because it's always in the news. One month it snaps up a competitor—or maybe a business in a wholly unrelated industry. The next month it shuts down a division and closes a bunch of factories. It's forever merging, acquiring, divesting, doing joint ventures, until pretty soon you'd be hard put to say what it does for a living. Maybe you've read Al Ries' book *Focus* (Harper Business, 1997), which argues that a successful enterprise must concentrate on its core business. These companies seem to have read some other book, which says to do the exact opposite.

Frankly, you can have that kind of fast company. It makes the investment bankers who engineer all the deals rich. Sometimes it makes the CEO rich, too. Investors and employees, however, rarely do so well. And you can forget about all the people who once had jobs in the businesses that no longer fit with the company's current strategy. They're out on the street. Mind you, I have nothing against buying and selling businesses. That's part of the free-enterprise system, and at PSS we have acquired dozens of companies over the years.

But if you can't *add value* to an acquisition—if all you're doing is shuffling assets in hopes of making a quick killing—then you aren't creating real wealth and opportunity. And your organization certainly doesn't deserve the title of *fast company*.

Then there's the kind of fast company that all the consultants and journalists love to write about. It's up on all the latest management fads and slogans. It's a virtual organization. It's knowledge-based. It's networked. It likes to think it doesn't really have a structure or an organization chart—it's just a collection of teams, of projects, of people solving problems. It isn't reengineered, it's *de*engineered.

This is not my idea of the ideal fast company. As a matter of fact, I've read a lot about these Information Age companies, but I've never met anybody who actually worked in one. If they really do exist—if you work in one—then God love them, and God love you. Maybe your organization is the wave of the future. Maybe you'll wind up putting the rest of us out of business. Meantime, we'll just have to earn our living making things, selling things, giving our customers what they seem to want. We'll operate the machines and answer the phones and drive the trucks and do all those other everyday-business types of things, and we'll hope we can get by until the Fourth Wave or the Fifth Wave or whatever wave we're on right now comes along and swamps our boats.

Okay, enough pontificating. I'll climb down off my soap box now and tell you what I think makes for a real fast company—a fast*er* company—in today's mercurial marketplace.

It's pretty simple. It's a company that knows where it is going and what it is doing. It's a company that can provide its customers with more value than they ever got before and more than they can get anywhere else—and can do so over and over, day in and day out.

Faster? This kind of company can spot changes in the marketplace and turn on a dime without losing its focus *or* its people. It can grow fast even in the most mature markets, and leave competitors wondering what happened. It can get things done fast because its people march to the same drum and don't need anybody looking over their shoulder telling them what to do. It doesn't do just a little better than the other guys, it does a whole lot better than the other guys. It leaves them in the dust.

You'll meet this kind of faster company in this book, and by the end you'll know exactly what goes into one. But PSS is hardly unique. Think for a moment about the organizations that have literally transformed whole sectors of today's economy, and you'll see examples of faster companies that fit my definition perfectly. Federal Express. Southwest Airlines. Wal-Mart Stores. Nucor, the steel company. These are the companies that make savvy investors (and many of their employees) rich. They are companies that revolutionized their industries—and decades later are still way out in front of everybody else. They fit today's marketplace the way Henry Ford's fit the early industrial age. They're the new blue chips.

This book is about how to create this kind of company. I'm going to start by telling you a little about PSS/World Medical and how it came to be. We'll go on to what I think are the four basic building blocks of any faster company—building blocks, moreover, that are missing from probably 95 percent of the businesses in the United States.

From there on, it's all hands-on implementation. You'll find 11 Commandments for actually creating a faster company, along with the tools and techniques we've developed at PSS to put these commandments into practice. This is where you get to the good stuff, like how we run a billion-dollar business with no policy manual, how you can take kids right out of college and turn them into a crackerjack sales force, and how to develop a bonus plan that gets warehouse workers thinking about managing their inventories better.

What all this amounts to, I believe, is a methodology—a methodology for building a company that no one can stop and that competitors just can't keep up with. I don't care what business you're in. I don't care where you are in an organization, whether you're the CEO or a junior employee just working his or her way up. If you get a chance to put these principles into action, you will wind up with a department, a business unit, or a company in which people reach levels of performance they never thought possible—and you'll all have one great time doing it.

PART ONE

The World's Nuttiest Billion-Dollar Company

"A Cross between the U.S. Marines and *Animal House*"

Funny thing about companies such as PSS/World Medical: At first glance, they don't look so different from other businesses. You could put any thriving enterprise into our shiny, glass-walled corporate headquarters on Southpoint Boulevard in Jacksonville, Florida. Other distribution companies would feel at home in our 106 branch facilities. We have warehouses and warehouse employees. We have delivery vans and people to drive them. We write paychecks just like everybody else, buy computers just like everybody else's, and send salespeople out to call on customers the way other businesses do. Our stock—the symbol is PSSI—is traded on NASDAQ, along with the shares of about a zillion other companies.

What's more, we're in an industry that's about as ordinary as they come. We distribute medical supplies to doctors' offices and nursing homes, and X-ray supplies to hospitals and radiology centers. Sure, some of what we carry is pretty fancy stuff: blood chemistry analyzers, bone densitometers, cardiac stress systems, and a lot of other big-ticket equipment that you need a medical degree to understand and use. But we don't manufacture this equipment, we just sell it. And most of what we sell—our day-in, day-out bread and butter—is a whole lot less complex. It's latex gloves, specimen containers, and wound dressings. It's needles and syringes, pregnancy test kits, and reagents for the diagnostic equipment. One of our biggest sellers is the toilet paper that doctors put in their bathrooms.

So why are you reading a book by a guy who heads up an ordinary-looking company in an everyday industry? Well, they say appearances deceive. And if you could come on a tour of PSS with me—a real behind-the-scenes and back-in-time tour, not a quickie first-glance-type tour—you would find yourself startled by just how *unordinary* this company is.

Maybe we could start our tour by dropping in on our St. Louis branch. Right now, they're doing fine. That's a good thing, because it wasn't so long ago that the employees of that facility felt that things weren't fine at all. That's when they decided to fire their leader.

Firing the boss isn't that unusual at PSS (see Chapter 14). Nor is it unusual for people throughout the organization to go over their superior's head—even if that superior happens to be the chief executive officer, and going over his head means going straight to the board of directors. The right to communicate with anyone, anywhere, without fear of retribution is one of the core values at PSS. Everybody knows it's a core value because it's right there on the Top 20 card that every employee carries in his or her wallet (see Chapter 6).

Then maybe we'd hop down to New Orleans and go out with one of our salespeople—Jennings Edney, say—as he calls on the physicians who are his customers. Note that Jennings doesn't carry an order book, he carries a little laptop computer with a pen-activated screen. That computer contains every snippet of information about Jennings's accounts that he might need to know. What they ordered in the past. Whether anything's on back order. The prices they paid, the equipment they expressed an interest in, and on and on.

See, we figure information is power—and we want to put power in the hands of our employees (see Chapter 11). In fact, a PSS truck driver such as Oleg Shkolyar carries a business card that says *Oleg Shkolyar, CEO*—because when PSS truck drivers are standing in a customer's office, they *are* CEOs. They have the absolute authority to do anything it takes to keep that customer happy (see Chapter 5).

Anyway, back to Jennings. Watch him when he leaves Dr. Smith's office. He hoists the little antenna on the radio-frequency transmitter attached to the computer. He hits a few keys. Presto: That order is now in the local warehouse, ready to be put on a truck for delivery that very afternoon. Same-day service—guaranteed for any customer within a 50-mile radius who places an order before noon—is what has always distinguished PSS from its competitors. We know how to do it and they don't, which means that we and they aren't really in the same business anymore. This is the kind of competitive edge that a really successful business absolutely must have, and that we're now replicating in wholly different branches of the health-care industry (see Chapter 4).

Let's move on. There are a few other people I'd like you to meet.

Charlie Alvarez is one. Charlie is vice president in charge of our northeast region. He oversees branches that rack up annual sales in the neighborhood of $110 million. He himself makes close to $200,000, including salary, bonus, and stock. Or at least he was making that much as I was writing this book; by now it's probably more. Charlie was born in 1967. You figure out how old he is.

Then there's Lorenzo. Lorenzo used to drive a truck in our Jacksonville branch. He drove a truck for PSS for more than ten years, and he never particularly wanted to move up in the organization. Then again, he hasn't done too badly. Last I looked, his employee stock account was worth more than $500,000. Maybe by now he's a millionaire.

And let's not forget Jim Boyd. Jim has been around almost since PSS was started and has done nearly every job in the organization. He has been a sales rep. He has opened up new branches and overseen acquisitions. He's been a regional officer. But it hasn't always been smooth for Jim; there were times when the job he was in just didn't work out. Funny thing, though: He's still here. He's a vice president of the company, and he's contributing mightily to PSS, in a job that's just right for him. He's bringing tremendous value to PSS and its shareholders. *Boy*, do I love this guy.

Of course, these people aren't exactly random selections. I chose them because I wanted to illustrate a few more of this company's unusual attributes.

- We give huge amounts of responsibility to people without much experience, many of them not long out of college. Charlie Alvarez is only one of many. That's a lesson I learned in Vietnam (see Chapter 5), and it has made a huge difference to PSS.

- We also believe in sharing the wealth—large amounts of wealth—with all our employees, through bonus plans and stock-ownership plans (see Chapter 15). We estimate that a couple of hundred people have already become millionaires through their ownership of PSS stock. Most of them have been employees.

- We challenge people to rise as far as they can in the organization. In fact, we almost always promote from within. But if things don't work out in any given job, as they didn't with Jim and many other people, they're entitled to a *soft landing* and the chance to try again (see Chapter 10).

Frankly, I'm not sure where else to take you on this introductory tour. We could go to the house I used to live in. That's where we all gathered one sunny day and buried a bank in the backyard. We even made a nice little tombstone. (For some choice thoughts about banks, bankers, and growing companies, see Chapter 2). We could sit in on a Challenge Game session at just about any branch. There, you'd see truck drivers and warehouse employees competing furiously to answer tough questions on PSS's financials and operations—even though the session is off-site, after hours, and purely voluntary. (You'll read about how we do it in Chapter 11). As we visited branch after branch, you'd probably notice that every one is virtually identical, right down to the P&L numbers that are posted on the wall for every employee to look at, and right down to the Wall of Fame that trumpets employee accomplishments. But I don't want to give away (yet) how we get this kind of crisp uniformity in a billion-dollar company with no policy manual, no rules and regulations, and damn few memos. For that you'll have to wait for Chapter 16.

What do all these funny ideas and practices add up to?

Part of the answer is that they add up to one helluva high-performance business. PSS started in 1983, with a single branch in Jacksonville. Five years later we had seven branches and $20 million in sales. That was enough to earn us a spot on the Inc. 500—the fastest-growing privately held companies in America. But while a lot of entrepreneurial companies hit a plateau at the $10 million or $20 million level, we never looked back. *Every year* after that, our sales grew 40, 50, or 60 percent. *Every year* after that, we added five or ten new branches. As I write, we're about to close a fiscal year in which our sales will top $1 billion.

When *Inc.* magazine wrote an article about us in 1995, the editors used the term *hypergrowth* to describe PSS's trajectory. In the years since the article appeared, our growth hasn't slowed one iota. As a matter of fact, it has actually accelerated since we went public in 1994.

Of course, sales growth is only one facet of a company's performance. If you were a Wall Street analyst, here are some other questions you'd want to have answered.

Do they make money? No fast-growing company is going to record huge profits, least of all in a distribution industry like ours. But we have lost money only once in our history. In fiscal 1997 we earned about $15 million (before charges for mergers) on revenues of nearly $700 million. But the significant fact here is how much Wall Street seems to like our long-term profit potential. We went public in 1994 at $3.67 a share (adjusted for a later three-for-one split). The stock rose steadily and has always been way above the offering price.

What about same-store sales? This is a question that all the pros want answered. In the retailing and distribution industries, same-store sales is a crucial measure. It tells you what's going on in your existing branches or outlets. Until you know that, you don't really know what accounts for the revenue growth. After all, a company could just be buying up other people's businesses, thus feeding the top line, and then running them into the ground. PSS's same-store sales, I'm happy to say, have grown at an annual rate of about 20 percent—more than *three times* the rate for the industry as a whole. In short, we have been swiping serious market share from the competition.

Okay, but what do they do for an encore? In 1997, PSS sold to about 55 percent of the 200,000 or so physician practices in the United States. Our market share of total dollars spent, though, was only around 15 percent. We're number one in the industry. But there's still plenty of room for growth—and being top dog helps rather than hinders. More and more manufacturers have been giving us exclusive rights to sell diagnostic equipment. Our size and focus give us buying power that competitors can't duplicate. And so far, no one has caught up with our ability to offer same-day delivery virtually anywhere in the country. So the competitive edge that helped us get where we are today is as sharp as ever.

We have also embarked on three other avenues of expansion. One is Europe. In 1997, we opened facilities in three European countries, and we'll see plenty more over there in the next few years. The second is sales and service of X-ray supplies and equipment, and the third—thanks to our recent acquisition of Gulf South Medical—is distribution of medical supplies to nursing homes. We have every expectation that our new divisions will be as successful, only faster, even though their competitive challenges are in some ways quite different.

From a growth-and-performance standpoint, in short, this is a company still in its infancy. If we could take that same company tour a decade from now, I'd bet you dollars to doughnuts that we'd find branches of PSS in a dozen different countries serving a dozen different sectors of the health-care industry. As you'll see in this book, we have created a company that can handle growth in a way that most businesses simply can't. So that's one thing that all our ideas and practices add up to.

But you know what? Despite Wall Street, despite the fact that this is a for-profit business, despite the fact that we all like to make money, financial performance really is only one measure of a company's success.

Think, for example, about your own company. Do you like to work there? Are people having fun, growing, and learning new things? Do they feel fairly treated and have a sense of belonging? Do they care what happens to the organization and go the extra mile to help it succeed?

At most businesses, the answer is *no*. And the *no* gets more and more pronounced as you move out beyond the people at the top. In fact, I've been in companies where I wouldn't even dare ask the hourly workers these questions. I'd be hooted off the shop floor.

At PSS, we have fun. We have more fun than I'd ever imagined a company could have. We have volleyball tournaments and picnics. We hold meetings at amusement parks, miniature golf arcades, and bowling alleys. We play games based on *Jeopardy!* and *Family Feud*. Every few months the headquarters staff—everybody—gets a little trip. We sent them to Key West. We hired a surfing instructor and got surfboards for everybody, then went to the beach. We visited an alligator farm and told them they'd be expected to wrestle an alligator. (Memo to our insurance company: Just kidding.) As for our annual sales meetings—well, frankly, they're a little over the top. We've been kicked out of nine hotels. Of course, I can't say that I blame the hotel folks. One day I arrived at a sales meeting to find a conference room strewn with bales of hay and outfitted with a mechanical bull. Seems that it was a little recreation someone had set up for between seminars. Believe me: The hotel staff was *not* happy.

But it isn't just fun that sets our culture apart, it's the feeling that I think everyone shares: This is *our* company. We belong. That's partly a matter of the tangible opportunities PSS provides, such as the opportunity to build real wealth and the chance for advancement to a better job. It's also a matter of the way we do things. First names throughout. No bureaucracy. The ability to say what you think to anybody, without fear of retribution. I don't mean to say that PSS is perfect, or even that it's for everybody. As you may have guessed, our culture is demanding. We hold each other strictly accountable for performance. Our standards are high. If you don't want to work hard, you won't make it here.

A while ago, someone characterized our company as a cross between the U.S. Marine Corps and *Animal House*. You know what the Marines stand for. If you haven't seen the old movie *Animal House*, don't bother—just hazard a guess. The title pretty much conveys the idea. So, incidentally, does the title of a recent book about Southwest Airlines: *Nuts*. I know Southwest is zany. I also know the folks there run a *great* company. But I'd stack PSS up against them on both counts. It says in that book that Southwest CEO Herb Kelleher once arm-wrestled a guy over a legal dispute rather than take it to court. Okay: I hereby challenge

Herb to an arm-wrestling match over who is nuttier—about performance, about having fun, about creating a company that *works* for its customers, its shareholders, and its people.

You know, none of this is rocket science. Sprinkled throughout this book you'll find a bunch of thank-yous. They're for the authors, the speakers, and the businesspeople all over the world whose ideas I have stolen. I don't think I've ever had an original idea in my life. At PSS, all the great ones were borrowed from somebody else, or were created by people working in a branch and then adopted by the whole company. What that means, of course, is that there's nothing magical about what we do. You can do it too. We have a saying at PSS, which we stole from the organization known as TEC (formerly The Executive Committee): *When you're green you're growing, and when you're ripe you're rotting.* Too many companies in America are ripe. They're slowly rotting on the vine. You can see it in people's faces. You can see it in the companies' performance. Who wants to work or invest in a place like that? A *green* company doesn't necessarily mean a small company or a new company. Nor does it mean you have to pursue the kind of hypergrowth that we've been lucky enough to experience. It just means a company in which the people are learning new things, expanding their horizons, finding new ways to serve their customers—and thus adding new customers all the time. Being in that kind of business really is fun. Being in the other kind of business just isn't much fun. This book will show you how to have fun.

I have to say, this wasn't exactly what we had in mind when we started out. When I was a kid in the Virginia Home for Boys, I just wanted to make it through the day. When I was pushed into starting my own business, my goal wasn't so different: I just hoped the business would survive. But maybe I'm getting ahead of myself. Let's go back to Houston, in 1983, and meet a guy named Buddy. Maybe my experiences with Buddy and a few other people will help you understand why things work the way they do at PSS.

Starting Out

They say that getting there is half the fun. I'd go one step far-
ther: Most journeys are more important and more fun than
arriving at the destination. That was certainly true of PSS.
But I sure didn't know what was in store the day my boss Buddy
called me into his office. That was the day I became a Reluctant
Entrepreneur. It was February 8, 1983. Nobody at PSS ever for-
gets the date, because every February 8 we celebrate Buddy Day
with cake and ice cream.

At the time, I was vice president of sales and marketing for a
company called Intermedco, headquartered in Houston. For me
it was a plum job, exactly the kind of position I'd hoped I'd be in
at that point in my career. I was 35 years old. My two daughters,
Mara and Jenny, were in elementary school. We had a nice house
and a couple of cars. We had just put in our first swimming pool.

Intermedco was a $41-million company, owned at that point by British Tire & Rubber (BTR). I figured my future looked pretty good. Starting a company was the last thing on my mind.

There was just one blemish on this otherwise rosy picture: According to the grapevine, our London bosses had decided to freeze the salaries of all of Intermedco's officers. No raise that year.

Now, this was aggravating. Intermedco's sales were up about 20 percent over the previous year. The company had made a profit for the first time in five years. I figured the other officers and I had contributed to this success. But BTR wasn't so sure. Buddy was president of the company—my boss—and I went to him to confirm the rumor that there would be no raises. He said that was right. I said I wasn't happy about it. I even said I might have to start looking elsewhere. Then I went back to my office.

A little while later, a guy named Bart, the vice president of operations, came into my office.

"Pat," he said. "Why did you quit?"

I looked up, surprised. "I didn't quit! I just said I was unhappy about not getting a raise and might have to look elsewhere."

"Oh, no," said Bart. "I think you quit."

We went back and forth like this for a couple of minutes. No, I didn't. Oh, yes, you did. Nothing that I said could persuade him otherwise, so I was left there scratching my head. Then Buddy walked in.

"I'd like your resignation today," said Buddy.

I shook my head. "Buddy, what is this? I am *not* quitting! I don't have a job to go to. If you want to fire me, go ahead. But I am not quitting."

Buddy's reply was emphatic. "Pat," he said, "we're not compatible." He then proceeded to spell out all the ways in which he thought we were not compatible.

Ouch! When your boss says to you that you and he aren't compatible, you have to face facts. Maybe you *are* quitting, after all. I called a friend in the industry, and he offered me a job in sales.

I flew to New York that night, and we made it official. Next day I did indeed hand in my resignation at Intermedco.

The next couple of months were tumultuous. I went to Florida to work for my new employer. My family stayed in Houston. The only constant amidst the tumult was the series of phone calls from an old friend of mine named Bill Riddell. Bill spelled out his agenda in the very first call.

"Hey," he said, "now that you've left Intermedco, let's start a company."

I *really* didn't want to start a company. Before going to Houston as vice president, I had worked for several years for Intermedco's Florida subsidiary, a company called Surgical Supply. I had a lot of friends from the years with Surgical Supply, including Bill, who was (and is) a world-class salesman. I didn't want to damage those relationships by starting a competitive business. But I had worked in the medical-distribution business my entire career, and that was the only kind of enterprise I was remotely qualified to start. Conclusion: no new company.

As the weeks went on, though, the new job proved pretty stressful. I wasn't exactly enamored of my new situation. I didn't know whether I'd wind up in Florida or Texas. If I moved my family again, I wanted the move to be permanent. And, always, there were those calls from Bill, sometimes three or four a week.

"Come on," he'd say. "Let's start a company." Or, "Hey, Pat, when are we going to start that company?"

Finally, at the end of April, I was attending a sales meeting in Houston. Something clicked. I had to put my life on a new track. I called Bill from that meeting and said, okay, okay, I'll come over and we'll talk about it. "But," I added, "you have to get at least one other sales rep to sign on."

Within ten minutes another sales rep, an old friend and colleague named Clyde Young, was on the phone. "If you come over here to start a company," he said, "I want to be part of it." On May 2, 1983, Physician Sales & Service (now PSS/World Medical) was born.

Starting a business has to be one of the crazier things we ever did. Maybe all entrepreneurs are crazy. Maybe you have to be to set up your own business. But I think our decision is right up there on the insanity scale.

For one thing, there were already hundreds of companies in the medical-distribution business. The industry was crowded, and the competition was fierce. I had already spent four years as general manager of one of our prospective competitors, Surgical Supply. Anything I knew about building a business I had already put into practice there. It's not as if I had any secrets up my sleeve.

For another thing, getting started in a distribution business is particularly difficult. It's a sales-driven industry, and no company wants to lose good salespeople. So you know you're in danger of being slapped with some kind of lawsuit every time you hire a sales rep away from a competitor. Then, too, manufacturers are reluctant to deal with an upstart. They have relationships with existing distributors and don't want to upset them. They also figure that the new kid on the block probably won't be around too long, so why get involved? Nearly every new distribution company has a hard time getting product to sell.

But there was one final wrinkle. This was the health-care business. And even in 1983, health-care companies were facing an uncertain future. In fact, the accounting firm Ernst & Whinney (now Ernst & Young) had been commissioned to do a study of the industry, and the study came out just about the time we were creating our company. There it was, in black and white. In years to come, said the study, health care would be dominated by eight or ten "supermeds." The supermeds would provide insurance. They would own hospitals and nursing homes. They would hire doctors or buy their practices. They'd buy up manufacturers and distributors of health-care products. They would own health care from cradle to grave.

So this was the environment. Everybody believed the era of

the small, independent company was over. Everybody thought we were nuts to be starting our own company. As I said, maybe we were. It would take hard work and good luck. Mostly, we figured, it would take tenacity—the ability to hang in there, take the inevitable blows, and get past the inevitable obstacles.

Tenacity, at least, was something I knew about. You see, I spent 13 years of my life, from ages 5 to 18, in the Virginia Home for Boys.

You'll read about the Boys Home a lot in this book. It's one of the oldest institutions of its kind in the country. You'll read about the men and women who raised me when my family couldn't, and about the lessons I learned there about how to treat people. My upbringing had a powerful effect on my ideas about how to run a business. But when you start a company, the only issue you care about is whether you'll survive. When I first got to the Boys Home, that was pretty much the only issue I cared about, too.

By 1952, my mother realized she needed help. I was five years old. My father had left the family right before I was born. My mother worked two or three jobs all the time, but the jobs didn't pay much. I was the third of three children. Sometimes she left me in the care of aunts, sometimes with my sister Jo Nell, who was eight years older and who kept me out of harm's way. The Boys Home was right in our neighborhood at that time, but the Home didn't ordinarily take boys until they were eight. Finally, with the help of our pastor, my mother persuaded the Home first to take my brother, Jimmy, at age six, and then myself, at age five. I was the youngest kid ever to live there.

The youngest—and the scrawniest.

I was a little red-faced Irish kid a good 20 or 30 pounds lighter than the next-smallest resident of the Home. And boys being boys, I took a pounding. Anytime someone had a lousy day, anytime someone was beaten up by a bigger kid, there was always somebody smaller that the loser of the last fight could beat up. Unfortunately, that someone was named Pat Kelly.

At some point—I'm not sure when—I realized I had to fight

back. Fists weren't much use against kids so much bigger. So I made a decision. Anytime a kid picked a fight with me, I'd grab him. I'd wrap my arms around him as best I could. Then I would sink my teeth into whatever part of his body was handiest. And keep them there.

Well, the kids howled. For a while, I probably got beaten up worse than I would have otherwise. But pretty soon word got around: You can beat that kid up, but he'll make you pay. Those bites *hurt*. And bit by bit, they stopped beating me up.

So when I decided to sink my teeth into starting a company, I wasn't planning on giving up any too easily.

Looking back on it, some of the hurdles we faced were exactly what we expected, only worse. Others were wholly unexpected, like the day the bank reneged on a loan we thought we already had. Some were the result of our own paranoia. A few were down-right ludicrous. One or two helped us make PSS a better company than it would have otherwise been. This book isn't really about how to start a business. But if you are starting one, or if you ever hope to, read on. You, too, may wind up under a desk, fearing that somebody has just lobbed a bomb into your brand-new office.

So the company's birthday was May 2, 1983. Its place of birth was Clyde's dining room table. There were four of us there: Bill Riddell, Clyde Young, a neighbor of mine, and me. My neighbor was interested in putting up some capital in return for a share of the equity. He and my two other partners all wanted an even split of the stock, 25 percent to each person. To tell the truth, I was a little apprehensive about that plan. It had already taken us a fair amount of time to work through the process of negotiating a deal. We knew I'd be the general manager—the chief executive—of the company. If I had an investor and two sales reps each owning 25 percent, I might have difficulty running things.

Fortunately, this initial obstacle yielded to what we still think was a pretty clever idea. I proposed a formula to the others. I would own 31 percent of the company. They'd each own 23 percent. That way, I'd have majority support for a decision if I could get just one of them to agree with me. If I couldn't sell at least one shareholder on an idea, then the chances were it wasn't a good idea. My partners bought the formula, and we shook on it. We were in business.

We had one other thing going for us: a clear conception of our market niche, and our competitive advantage. If we failed, it wouldn't be because we didn't know what we wanted to do.

At that time, the companies that supplied physicians' offices typically sold not just to doctors but to hospitals and nursing homes. They liked large orders. They'd load up their big trucks with pallets full of product. They might visit the physicians' offices once every few weeks and drop off a bunch of cartons. It would be the doc's problem to figure out where to store them. And if the office ran out of syringes or wound dressings between deliveries, well, that was tough luck—mostly for the nurse who got blamed for not ordering enough.

Our company, we decided, would be called Physician Sales & Service. Yes, we took a lot of ribbing about the name. ("You sell doctors?") But it reflected our focus. We would sell *only* to doctors' offices. We'd take an order and deliver it the very next day in a spiffy PSS van. We would provide a level of service that doctors and nurses had never experienced. In turn, we would be able to charge a little bit more than the bulk suppliers charged.

It would prove to be a good idea. If only we could jump those hurdles and swim those moats.

Obstacle 1: Getting Product

We cut the deal on a Friday morning. Bill and Clyde were fired that day. I resigned. We had figured we'd give two weeks' notice, but Surgical Supply, their employer, suspected they were going into business for themselves and fired them on the spot. So I had to quit right away, too. We had no inventory, no building, no nothing. Bill and Clyde sat down and made up a list of the products they needed. We called a medical distributor I knew up in Atlanta and arranged to buy inventory from him. That weekend, Bill and Clyde drove a U-Haul all the way to Atlanta to pick up the products, while I scouted around for a building. Saturday afternoon we found one. Sunday, Bill and Clyde came back with their inventory. We didn't have any shelving, so we laid it out on the floor. Monday morning, Bill and Clyde were out on the street soliciting orders and calling them in. We hired a kid we knew as a truck driver and gave him my car to make the deliveries. It wasn't until Tuesday that we could find a truck.

Whew! We did $23,000 worth of business that first month. Getting the orders wasn't so hard; Bill and Clyde were skilled, experienced sales reps and had good relationships with their customers. Filling the orders—and making money—was something else again. The Atlanta supplier couldn't provide us with everything we needed, so we had to scour the countryside for other distributors. We had no access to big manufacturers such as Johnson & Johnson, so we had to make do with lesser-known brand names. Our margins were tight. Our Atlanta supplier, for example, probably paid about 5 percent more for product than our competitors did. We bought from him at cost plus 10 percent, so we were at a 15 percent disadvantage right out of the gate. And despite what we might claim about our service, we couldn't start out with higher prices. We'd have to earn the right to charge more than the other guys.

So we scrambled. Boy, did we scramble. Surgical Supply was a good company, but they had a problem with back orders. We felt if we could keep our back orders to an absolute minimum, we could make an impression on the customer. Over and over, we had product shipped to us overnight so we could deliver it the next day, and to hell with the expense. If overnight delivery wasn't available, we figured out something else. At one point, one of Bill's customers had six pairs of crutches on order and told Bill in no uncertain terms that if they didn't get the crutches the next day she was calling Surgical Supply. We had already ordered the crutches, but back then UPS wouldn't ship big parcels overnight, so it was going to take three days to get them. Not soon enough. I wound up driving to three different drug stores around Jacksonville and buying six pairs of crutches at retail. They cost us $30 a pair, and we had to deliver them to Bill's customer at $9 a pair. It sort of set a precedent for us: Get the product at all cost. We'll worry about things like price and margin down the road.

If there was going to be a down the road. Because right about then came the lawsuits.

Obstacle 2: Lawsuits

Intermedco, parent of Surgical Supply, made a quick strategic decision when they got wind of what we were up to. They were big. They had a London parent, British Tire & Rubber, with deep pockets. I think they were worried that the three of us would grab hold of a piece of the market. So they followed that good old American competitive strategy: Sue the bastards. Of course, none of us had noncompete agreements. We hadn't violated any laws or ethical principles that we knew of. It didn't matter. They sued us for taking confidential information. They sued us for stealing proprietary processes. They sued the company. They sued us as individuals. They sued us in Florida. They sued us in Texas. I'm sure their thinking was pretty simple. We'd go broke fighting their lawsuits. They wouldn't go broke. End of story.

As it happened, they were right about one thing. If we had to fight all those lawsuits to the bitter end, we probably would have gone broke. We started the company with only $40,000 in equity. But they hadn't quite counted on our tenacity. We had a board member, a neighbor of mine named Fred Elefant, who was a lawyer. We explained the situation to Fred and begged him for help. Not only was Intermedco suing us, I said, I also felt they were pressuring manufacturers not to sell to us.

If you're starting a company, I strongly recommend you find a lawyer like Fred. Fred went to his law firm and presented our case. He argued that PSS had a counterclaim against Intermedco—tortious interference and an antitrust claim—and would be a strong candidate to collect punitive damages. The partners in the law firm liked his argument and agreed to take our case on contingency. We'd pay the first $10,000 worth of legal bills. They'd be responsible for everything after that. If we won, we'd split the proceeds 50-50.

So we went toe-to-toe with Intermedco in every court and every situation. It got more and more complicated. In our countersuit, we named several manufacturers as coconspirators, and they all had to be deposed. It was very costly. I can't imagine what Intermedco was thinking. See, they didn't know we had a contingency arrangement with the law firm. They must have been wondering where all the money was coming from.

Anyway, one day we're in New York City to interview a manufacturer. Intermedco shows up with three lawyers. The meter's running on these lawyers—back then, it was maybe $100 or $125 an hour. Plus they're staying at the fanciest hotel in town. We were there for three days.

On the third day, my old pal Bart, who was still Intermedco's VP of operations, says, "Pat, come out in the hall and let's talk." Once in the hall he asks me how I think the suit's going.

I'm not sure what to make of the question. After all, he's the guy who's suing me. But I don't blink. "Seems to me it's going just fine, Bart."

"Yeah, but aren't you nervous about all the money you're spending?"

"Bart, we're not spending any money. We've got this on contingency. The only money we're spending is for my hotel room. But hey—I'm having a good time. Tell me, have you been to see this new play on Broadway?"

Bart looks at me, dumbfounded. "This is on contingency?"

"Oh, yeah," I say, as nonchalantly as I can. "They think

they've got a good enough case to win in Florida. An antitrust case. And by the way, punitive damages are three times the actual damages."

"Oh," says Bart. He looks as if he wants to melt into the floor.

Before we left New York, Intermedco wanted to settle. They paid all our legal fees up to that point, including our $10,000. We agreed not to hire any of their employees for a year. Fred Elefant's firm got about $100,000, and we got our biggest legal problems behind us. A year later, we hired three of their sales reps in Orlando, Florida. As I write, those three reps—Todd, Ken, and Joe—are still selling for PSS in Orlando and are three of our top reps in the whole country.

Things like lawsuits and depositions lead to a certain kind of paranoia. Maybe you could call it entrepreneurial paranoia. We felt like there was this big bully trying to keep us out of his territory. Who knew what he'd stop at? Your mind does nutty things. One night, for example, Clyde and I were sitting at a desk in PSS's original office doing paperwork. All of a sudden a truck wheels into the parking lot, tires screeching. A guy reaches out the window and throws something against our front door.

"Clyde!" I yell. "It's a bomb!"

I dive under the desk. Clyde dives under his desk. After a couple of minutes—of course—nothing has happened. We look at each other. He says, "Pat, I don't think it's a bomb." We go to the front door and open it. It's a weekly newspaper, a shopper. The truck was delivering newspapers.

It gets worse. We had word from people in the industry that Intermedco was accusing me of stealing confidential information and that the authorities in Texas had issued an arrest warrant for me. My family was still in Texas, though, and I wanted to visit them over the Fourth of July holiday. I booked a flight under an assumed name. When I got to the Houston airport I felt like a spy, sneaking incognito down the corridors.

Some spy. Suddenly I hear on the PA system, "Would Pat Kelly please pick up courtesy phone number three?" I look around, figuring it's a trick. No way I'm going to fall for that. But five minutes later there's the same message again. I figure they've got my wife, Judy, and my daughters, Mara and Jenny. I might as well give up. When I do pick up the phone, it's Judy.

I say, "Where are you?"

She says, "I'm in a phone booth! The car broke down."

I say, "I'm trying to sneak into town incognito, and *you have me paged at the airport? Wow!*"

Oh, well. No police showed up. I never did find out if the rumor about an arrest warrant was true. But I did realize I was getting pretty nutty. If you have ever started a company, maybe you recognize the feeling. On the other hand, some of what we ran up against was enough to drive anybody crazy. When we started out, for example, we dutifully figured out how much state sales tax we owed on our first month's revenues. Then we made out a check to the State of Florida and mailed it in.

Before long, the check came back. Since we didn't have a tax ID number, they couldn't take our money.

We checked to be sure our application for an ID number was in. By now we had recorded two months' worth of sales, so we voided the first check, wrote out a larger one, and sent it in, along with a note explaining that our application for an ID number was pending.

Didn't work. The State of Florida sent this check back, too. No tax ID number.

I got on the phone. I talked to clerks and their supervisors and their supervisors' supervisors. It isn't that we really love paying money to the government. But we knew we'd have to at some point, and it just drove us nuts that the state didn't have its act together. Nothing we did gave me any satisfaction, however. If we didn't have a number, they couldn't take our money.

Probably you can see the punch line of this story coming. In due course we got our number. We sent in a check for what was now three months' worth of back taxes that we owed.

Sure enough: Pretty soon we got a notice that we had been delinquent in paying our taxes for the first three months, and we owed a penalty. I called the Department of Revenue in Tallahassee and explained the whole situation, including the checks that had been returned to me. Their answer was short and to the point: "What kind of idiot would start a company without a tax ID number?"

Rather than argue, we wrote out a check. We had no stomach to fight over such an insignificant issue. We figured we had more important things to do, like building a business.

As the saying goes: Just because you're paranoid doesn't mean they aren't out to get you. When you're an entrepreneur, people *are* out to get you. Intermedco and others want to protect their business against competition. The state wants your money (so long as you have all the right paperwork). Then there are some investors, and a bank that I'd better not name, who have trouble with the risk involved. Happily, the little problem with our investor and the bank worked out pretty well. It made PSS a stronger company than it would have otherwise been.

Our first year in Jacksonville had been remarkably successful, despite the lawsuits. Bill and Clyde brought in a lot of business. Another sales rep, Mike McCoy, joined us. Then, four months into our startup, four seasoned sales reps approached us as a group; they, too, wanted to sign on. We jumped at the opportunity. When the year was over, we had done $1.7 million in revenues, and were even showing a profit. Of course, the three partners didn't make much. We each earned only $23,000 that year, as compared with the salary about three times higher that I had been earning at Intermedco.

A company that starts off this fast, however, has one big problem. It's called *cash*.

Obstacle 3: Cash

Every entrepreneur will recognize the problem. You're spending on salaries. You're spending on building up inventory. We had started the business with an initial investment of only $100,000, including $40,000 in equity and $60,000 in debt. Most of the debt had come from our investor, my neighbor. In addition, he had personally guaranteed a $100,000 line of credit at the bank.

Right: That's the bank I'm not going to name. I still do business in the same town. It's the bank that we would bury a little while later.

When those four salespeople joined us, we needed still more cash. Our investor guaranteed another $100,000 on our credit line at the bank. This was a good thing, because without it we wouldn't make payroll. I went down to the bank and arranged with the loan officer to draw on the line and deposit the money in our payroll account. I put the deposit slip—it was for $50,000—in my pocket and walked out of the bank.

That's when the banker comes running down the street after me. "Pat," he shouts. "I need to see you a minute."

Sure, I say. We go back in and sit down in his office. I was expecting him to thank me for giving him our business.

Instead, he reaches across the desk and into my shirt pocket. Then he pulls out the deposit slip. He says, your investor has just called up and withdrawn his support, so the extra credit line is no good. He tells me he's taking back the $50,000 I thought I had just deposited in my account.

I can't believe my ears. It doesn't occur to me until later that this might not be exactly legal on the banker's part. All I can think is, how the hell are we going to make payroll? This is the first payday after those four reps joined us. If we don't make payroll, they're likely to be out of here tomorrow.

So I go get Bill and Clyde. Together we figure how much we have in our personal accounts, and withdraw all we can. There's just enough to pay everybody. All the employees get their checks. Except us. We knew we could live on credit cards for a while if we had to.

Now it's time to talk to our investor. I call him and ask if I can come over and see him. He meets me at the door of his office and shows me in.

I ask him why he pulled his support for the line at the bank.

Well, he says, he has been thinking. He's been talking things over with another neighbor of ours. And he just feels that he shouldn't have so much money tied up in a company where he owns only 23 percent of the stock. He feels he should have a bigger ownership stake.

I ask him how much of a stake he has in mind. His answer is about what I expect: 51 percent.

At that point I felt I didn't have much of a choice about what to do. I reminded him that he had given his word that he would back this venture and told him I felt he had gone back on his word. I said that he now owned 23 percent of PSS but that in a little while he would own none whatsoever. I said we'd have to part company and that I would have someone buy out his stock within 30 days.

Then I walked out the door. I was sweating, and my knees were knocking together. I had no clue where I would find somebody to buy out that stock.

Just as I was getting in my car, he came out. "Pat," he said, "let's talk about this." We went back in, and he apologized. He said yes, he had made a commitment, and he would live up to it. He'd call the bank and renew his support. But, he added, we needed to raise more equity.

The fact was, I couldn't agree more. If the bank was willing to renege on a commitment at the wave of the investor's hand, we were obviously on shaky financial footing. I had gotten the same advice from a friend in the industry that I had been talking to not long before. If you're running a fast-growth company, he had said, you need to build your equity. He added that you really should have a quarter of a million dollars in equity to start a medical-distribution company.

For a long while I had believed in the idea that employees of a company should be shareholders in that company. It seemed to me just like common sense: Everybody's an owner, everybody benefits if the company succeeds. So we thought maybe we should ask PSS's employees—there were 21 at the time—to put up at least a portion of the money we needed. At the same time, I was worried we would create an expectation that PSS would be a democracy. No company can be a pure democracy, especially when starting up. A company in a high-risk startup situation like ours needs a firm hand at the controls. It was tough enough to get four partners to agree on major moves. I didn't want to have to convince 21 shareholders every time we wanted to open up a new branch or take on a new product line.

The idea we came up with was so simple it was unreal. We went to all the employees and said, we're going to sell stock in this company at one dollar a share. The book value of the common stock was only ten cents at the time, but this would be non-voting preferred stock. "If we blow it," I said, "if we don't make it, then you're in line right behind the banks. And there's a good chance you'll get your money back.

"But," I added, "if we do make it, we'll give you two choices. At the end of three years you can cash out. You can sell this stock back to the company, and we'll give you everything you invested plus ten percent per year return. If you decide you want to keep your stock, we'll convert it to common stock."

The employees were enthusiastic. Every single one got together whatever funds he or she could come up with. Many even borrowed on their homes or from their relatives. All told, we raised $152,000 from our 21 employees. Put that together with our existing $40,000 in equity and we were well on our way to the quarter-million my friend said we needed.

I guess the startup phase of our company-building process had a happy ending. A series of happy endings.

PSS continued to grow. By 1987, we had several branches in Florida and 120 people on the payroll. Only four years old, we were well established in the industry.

Our investor and I got back together and worked out our disagreement. He invested more money in PSS stock, and until recently had never sold a share.

When the three years were up, none of the employees asked for their money back. They all converted their preferred shares to common shares. We set up an employee stock-ownership plan and several other mechanisms by which people could buy shares. That put us on the road to being an employee-owned company—with all the benefits that you'll read about in later chapters.

The bank? Well, maybe the bank wasn't such a happy ending. Except we made it into one.

As I said, a fast-growing company needs cash. We always needed cash, and we were constantly outrunning our credit line. We were asked to leave four banks for growing too fast. I have come to the conclusion that banks aren't really in the business of lending money, they're in the business of generating fees. They lure you in, sign you up, and collect their up-front fees on your loan. Then they turn you over to a loan officer whose goal is to get rid of you. Fortunately for us, we finally locked on to a national bank that has helped us continue to grow.

Naturally, we left the bank that had reneged on the loan just as soon as we could. But a few years later, somehow, they enticed us back. And then they kicked us out again.

Frankly, I couldn't believe I could have been so stupid. I told my staff, we are going to *bury* this bank.

I said bury, and I meant *bury*. First we got some of our people to build a casket and a tombstone. Then we shut down the office for a day. We took every file, every brochure, every coffee cup and golf ball that we could find that had this bank's name on it, and we put them into the casket. Then we all went over to my house on the banks of the St. Johns River and dug a grave. We lowered the casket into it. But I can't say we were too sad. People were hooting and hollering. It was less like a funeral than like an independence party. Never again would we let ourselves be duped by this bank!

Still, you have to note what we didn't do.

After the burial, Shelly, one of our office employees, came up to me and said, "Pat, it's such a beautiful day, why didn't we get on your boat and have a burial at sea?"

"That's a great idea, Shelly," I replied, "but let me explain to you why we didn't. Some day we may need that bank, and I'm going to have to kiss that bank's ass. So I want to know where to come and dig up the casket."

In business, you never want to burn your bridges. You just want to learn from your mistakes. We managed to learn from most of them, and we were lucky enough to be able to create a small but successful entrepreneurial business. Maybe we could have stayed right there, with $10 million or $20 million in sales and 100 or 200 employees. Many fine companies do.

But I think we all had something else in mind. Something not just bigger but more ambitious. We wanted to keep on growing and, in the process, to build not just a larger company but a better one. We wanted to create a *great* company, a company that could reshape its industry and provide opportunities that people never expected, a company that could let us all realize our dreams. Isn't that what business at its best is all about?

Thank you, Buddy. Without Buddy, maybe none of this would have happened.

PART TWO

Four
Building Blocks
of a Faster
Company

CHAPTER 3

Gutsy Goals

M ost companies are pretty ordinary. People come in, do their job, and go home. Products are made and sold, services are delivered. New initiatives—if there are any—are greeted with shrugs and yawns. The prevailing attitude among employees: *It's just a job* (or It's not *my* job). The mindset among executives and managers: *I'll stay here for a few years until something better comes along.*

But there are a few companies that stand out from the pack. They do things differently. They move fast, change fast, and perform at a level that others can't begin to match, so they leave the competition in the dust. The people at these companies feel proud, even privileged, to work there. They go the extra mile to help the business succeed. I mentioned a few of my favorite examples in the introduction: Federal Express, Southwest Airlines, Wal-Mart, and Nucor. You can probably name others. Intel is certainly one. Dell Computer is another.

What makes a company stand out like this? What traits enable it to achieve and sustain a seemingly impossible level of performance—a level that competitors can't seem to attain—year after year after year?

I think there are only four of these traits. They're the four building blocks of a faster company.

- *Standout companies have a goal.*   They're focused. They know exactly where they're going.

- *Standout companies have a real competitive edge.*   They know how to do things—to deliver value to customers—that their competitors don't.

- *Standout companies allow people to perform at the level they're capable of.*   Believe me, that level is *much* higher than most people perform in most organizations.

- *Standout companies stand for something.*   They have values, and those values permeate the entire organization.

This chapter and the three following chapters will show you how we built PSS/World Medical around each of these building blocks. But I'll repeat what I said earlier.

We aren't unique. These are time-tested ideas. The best companies understand them. The question for your company isn't *whether* you should implement them but *how soon*. Nobody at PSS considers himself or herself a genius. Nobody graduated from an Ivy League college or got an MBA from some fancy business school. If we could do it, you can too.

By 1988, PSS was a successful entrepreneurial company. We had grown to seven branches and $20 million in sales. We had nearly 150 employees. Granted, we weren't making much money—only

$239,000 on those $20 million in revenues, for a whopping return on sales of 1.2 percent. But we were growing fast, and growth is always expensive. In general, we were proud of what we had accomplished. We even made the 1988 Inc. 500. PSS was number 302 on the magazine's list of the fastest-growing privately held companies in the United States.

And how did we get there? The same way a lot of young companies do. Hard work. Good people. Seat-of-the-pants navigation. A lot of luck. We didn't really understand the building blocks—or if we did, we couldn't have put it into words.

It was right about then that Charles Garfield asked me if I knew what our company's goal was.

Okay, so he didn't ask me directly. He asked me and a lot of other people.

Garfield—author of *Peak Performers* (Avon Books, 1991) and other books—was the keynote speaker at a conference in Milwaukee for Inc. 500 companies. And he was blunt. "I bet you all have mission statements for your companies," he told the audience. "I also bet they're mostly just a bunch of platitudes that nobody pays attention to." You could see the heads nodding in agreement.

Then Garfield delivered his message. Mission statements, he said, just don't cut it. "If you don't have a *goal* for your company—a goal that you can describe in a phrase or a sentence— you really don't know where you're going." And if you don't know where you're going, your company will always be buried somewhere in the middle of the pack, along with all the other companies that don't really know where they're going.

Garfield's message hit me like a ton of bricks, because I was just starting to realize something. I wasn't sure where we were going.

Growing up in the Boys Home, my objectives were always clear. I wanted the things I didn't have. New clothes, instead of the hand-me-downs we all wore. Money in my pocket. The chance to make something of myself. Of course, I was young, and like a lot of young people I didn't always have my priorities straight. All through high school, for example, I had two goals. I wanted to go to college. My brother Jimmy was going to college, the first kid in our time from the Home to do so. I figured if he could, so could I—and besides, college seemed like the best route to the economic opportunity we all wanted. But mostly I wanted a car. More than anything else I wanted a car. For years, I saved nearly everything I earned from working afternoons and weekends at the local Safeway and doing extra jobs around the Home. At 18, I actually walked into a local dealership and paid $3,600 cash for a hot-red Pontiac Le Mans 4-speed 287. Meantime, I had indeed been accepted at Virginia Commonwealth University, so it seemed like both my dreams were about to be realized.

If only it were so easy! I did indeed go off to college in 1965 in my new car, free from the constraints of the Home. But once there, I found I had a new goal: having fun. That first semester, my new car and I had a *lot* of fun. We rarely went to class, but we sure did have fun.

At the end of the first semester, I got my grades. I think I had a couple of Ds and three Fs. Things went downhill from there. Second semester, I failed all of my courses except German. I got a D in German only because the professor made me a deal: She'd pass me, just so long as I agreed never to take another course in German. The dean called me in for a little chat. Suddenly I was on the fast track out of Virginia Commonwealth University. So much for my goal of going to college.

Or so it seemed. In fact, I just had a little growing up to do. Soon I was drafted, got married, and was sent to Vietnam. When I returned from overseas, I understood a little more about the importance of an education. I went back to that same dean and told him I wanted to reenter VCU when I got out of the service.

He got out my grades and looked at them. He kind of chuckled. Then he told me, in effect, that hell would freeze over before he'd let me back in.

I begged. I pleaded. Before, I said, I had been young and stupid. I didn't know any better. Now here I was, a Vietnam vet, a married man. Couldn't he see his way to giving me another chance?

Finally, we came to a compromise. He told me to take two courses during the eight months I had left in the service. If I got Bs, he'd let me back in. "But Pat," he added, "if you don't make straight Bs in the first semester here, I'll bounce you out so fast you won't know what hit you."

I said, "Sir, if I don't have straight Bs in the first semester, you won't have to kick me out. I'll quit."

That was the last time in my young life that I needed to have anyone spell out my objectives for me. I took those two courses at Troy State, in Alabama, while I finished up my stint in the army, and earned an A in both. I returned to VCU and completed a four-year premed program in two and a half years, with almost straight As. It wasn't that I was so smart. Heck, I didn't have any more native intelligence than I had before, when I flunked out. But there was a *big* difference: I finally knew where I was going. And if you know where you're going, you can accomplish a lot. *It's not how smart you are, it's how you apply yourself that determines your success.*

That's pretty much how it was for the first 15 years of my career. After college, I realized I didn't really want to go to medical school. I was a married man with a baby on the way. I wanted to get a job and make some money. So I joined a company called General Medical, which was in the medical-distribution business. Later, I left General Medical to go to work for Intermedco. At both companies, I'd set goals for myself. At the end of two years, I wanted to be making so much money. At the end of three years, I wanted to be in such-and-such a position. When I reached a goal, I'd set another. Keeping my eye on the ball like that helped me attain the position of vice president of sales and marketing at Intermedco at age 35.

When Bill, Clyde, my neighbor, and I started PSS, our goals were equally simple and straightforward. You might say they were the entrepreneurial equivalent of climbing the corporate ladder. First, we wanted the company to survive. Then, we wanted to get our incomes back to where they had been before we started the business. Once the company was successful, we wanted to make money. We figured that's what it was all about: making money. If you made money you could have all the stuff you wanted.

But by 1988, we were making plenty of money.

We were running a $20-million company, each of us earning a nice salary. If we ever sold the company, we'd net a few million. We had nice homes, boats, a couple of cars apiece. Did we really want more money? For myself, I didn't know what I would spend it on. So what were our goals, anyway? These were the questions we were asking ourselves when Charlie Garfield came along and asked me what my company's goal was. I started thinking, maybe what we all needed was a new challenge. Something big. Something no one had ever done before.

When I came back from Milwaukee, I had an idea: that PSS could become the first national physician-supply company.

The first national physician-supply company? I can hear people's reactions to this goal as if it were 1988 right now. *Are you nuts? Pat, we're just a little-bitty company in Florida.* The younger employees looked at me like I was on drugs. My partners sort of rolled their eyes. Bill, in particular, thought the idea was crazy.

I had to admit, it was nothing if not a big challenge. Here we were, a successful but still very small company. All our branches were in a single state. We were a bit player in a multi-billion-dollar industry. Many companies were much larger—my old employers General Medical and Intermedco, for example. To my colleagues, it was as if the coach of a pretty fair small-college basketball team had just announced that the team's goal was to make it to the Final Four of the NCAA tournament. Or maybe not just make the Final Four but to win the whole darn thing. Watch out, Duke. Watch out, Kentucky. Here comes Podunk U.

And yet, the fact was that there was no national physician-supply company. The big national players supplied hospitals and nursing homes as well as physicians. The distributors that focused on physicians' offices were mostly small, mom-and-pop operations. One by one, I talked to people and sketched out a vision of the future. (*Visualize* your goal, said Charlie Garfield.) This was an industry ripe for consolidation. Whoever got out there first could acquire some of those small distributors and push others out of the business. If it wasn't PSS, it would be someone else. But why shouldn't it be PSS? We had a proven track record. We had shown that we could compete successfully with anybody, including companies considerably bigger than ourselves. If we took on the challenge, there would be opportunities for everybody—opportunities to learn, grow, travel, and make a ton of money besides.

And, one by one, people began to buy into this vision. Soon it was the company's official goal. We put big banners up in every branch announcing that we would be the first national physician-supply company. We put the phrase on every company document. Every meeting, we'd mention it. Every time the other officers and I visited a branch, we'd talk to people about what it meant. In a few months, every single employee in PSS could tell you exactly what the company's goal was.

And what we found was just what Garfield had promised: Having a goal transforms a company.

How so? We counted four ways—but the fact is, we're still discovering new advantages every day.

Advantage 1: A Bold Goal Sets You Apart from the Pack

Most businesses don't have goals. Oh, I know, the CEOs of publicly traded companies periodically issue pronouncements about their objectives: so much growth in sales, so much growth in earnings per share, whatever. But these aren't *goals*. Real goals have to do with achieving something meaningful, something that gets people's juices flowing. To go back to that basketball analogy, you don't hear coaches telling players that their goal for this game is to take five percent more shots or commit three percent fewer fouls. Teams play to win. It's the same with companies. Jack Welch of General Electric says that his goal is to have every one of GE's divisions be number one or number two—preferably number one—in its marketplace. Now, that's a *goal*. If a division isn't there, it has to get there. If it is there, it has to stay there. If it can widen the lead over whoever is next in line, so much the better.

When PSS established its goal, people in the industry began to notice us. Maybe they thought we were nuts, but they sure knew our name. When we began making our first acquisitions, we'd say to the salespeople and truck drivers of the companies we were acquiring, stick with us. We're going to be the first national physician-supply company. You'll have the opportunity to be part of something special. Suddenly, PSS wasn't just another little company in the medical-supply business. It was that upstart out of Florida—the one with all the big ambitions.

Advantage 2: A Bold Goal Fires Up the Troops

Ever seen chief executives and division managers try to motivate their people? They'll stand up and give fiery speeches about serving the customer and beating the competition and building this great company. When they're done, the employees file out, snickering. Then they go back to doing whatever they were doing before.

And why shouldn't they? After all, if you don't know where you're going, who cares how fast you get there?

It's different when you have a goal. Goals, by definition, are measurable. You can see progress toward them. When the CEO stands up to motivate the troops, he or she can point to tangible accomplishments. If you have a big goal, suddenly it *matters* whether you hit this year's objectives, because if you don't you're no longer on track for the Big Goal—and you're in danger of falling back into the middle of the pack again.

Then, too, every company has its share of ambitious young people who want to achieve something, make their mark, and get ahead in the organization. If there's no goal, all this energy and talent goes in a thousand different directions. People aren't quite sure what's most valued in the organization. They make their best guesses and hope their choices turn out to be right. They play politics, hoping to get noticed by someone influential. It's like the way things work in a peacetime army. Nobody's quite sure what the organization's priorities are, so nobody's quite sure what they have to do to get ahead.

A company with a goal, in contrast, is like a wartime army. There will be differences about strategy and tactics, sure. But no one can have a shred of doubt about what the objective is. And everyone knows that anything contributing to that objective will be valued. When PSS set out to be the first national physician-supply company, our young hotshots knew that if they could open up a new territory, they'd be furthering our goal, and they'd be sure to be noticed.

Funny thing: We didn't really have any trouble finding people to do just that.

Advantage 3: A Goal Keeps You Focused

I love that book by Al Ries called *Focus* (HarperBusiness, 1997). It reminds you of something smart companies know: You have to concentrate on what you do best. A lot of organizations forget this. They get seduced by what looks like a hot new opportunity. They decide it's time to diversify. Pretty soon they're in a business they don't know anything about. Worse, their customers start to get confused about what business they're in. Remember a few years ago when United Airlines decided it really should be a diversified travel company? United bought into the hotel and rental-car businesses and renamed itself Allegis Corp. Fortunately, someone came along who had better sense and refocused the company on the airline business before it went down the tubes.

When a marketplace is changing rapidly, focus is critically important. You can see it in health care, which is changing about as fast as any industry you can think of. One market shrinks while another expands. New players try to elbow their way in. In our industry, most of our competitors were bought, sold, or merged—sometimes more than once—in the space of just a few years. Pharmaceutical distributors have been nosing their way into the medical-supply business. If we didn't have a goal, PSS could easily have lost its way. We'd have been asking ourselves: Should we get into supplying nursing homes? What about hospitals? Maybe we should get into a different kind of distribution business altogether? We wouldn't have been the first company to abandon what we were good at in hopes of finding greener pastures somewhere else. Today we *are* in different segments of health-care distribution—but each unit is separate and focused on its core customer needs.

So the goal made a big difference. We were going to be the first national physician-supply company. If a strategic move didn't contribute to reaching that goal, we wouldn't even consider it. The goal of being the first national physician-supply company had to be achieved before we could consider anything else.

Advantage 4: A Goal Makes Decisions Easy

Even within your own market niche, it's easy to get bogged down in uncertainty. Should we expand into Texas? What about the Northeast? Should we be going after venture capital? Every chief executive must make a hundred strategic decisions every year, and it's easy to get muddled. A goal clarifies the options. At PSS, we couldn't say that we were going to be a national company except for Texas, or except for the Northeast. We couldn't say that we would be a national company except we didn't have enough capital. We had to make all those things happen.

Ultimately, however, the importance of a goal lies in what happens when you achieve it. That's when the goal-setting process helps you take the company to the next higher level.

Once we set our goal of going national, we took off. We grew from 7 centers in 1988 to 20 in 1990 and 25 in 1991. We had sold $2 million worth of equity to a venture-capital firm, Tullis-Dickerson Co., in 1989, and we leveraged that so we had more cash for acquisitions and expansion. Between 1991 and 1993, we added 15 new branches. In 1994, we took the company public and raised nearly $16 million in new equity; late the following year, we went back to the public markets in a secondary offering and raised another $142 million. In 1995, we bought one of our largest competitors, Taylor Medical. Thanks to the acquisition, we had 54 facilities at the end of fiscal 1995, spread throughout the United States. We were indeed the first national physician-supply company. So far, we're the only one.

But what do we do for an encore?

We began thinking about that as far back as 1993, when it looked as if our first goal was within reach. We knew we wanted another big challenge, something to get people fired up. We didn't really care if it seemed out of reach—after all, the goal of being a national company had seemed out of reach, too. What's the point of setting a goal if it isn't going to be something ambitious?

That year, we began talking to our people about a new goal: Could we become a billion-dollar company? Could we reach $1 billion in revenues by, say, the year 2001?

Now this, too, was pretty crazy. When we announced the goal, we had maybe $170 million in revenues. A few of our investors thought we were nuts. Inside PSS, though, we noticed a different reaction. Sure, people were a little bug-eyed at the size of the goal. On the other hand, not many people thought we couldn't do it. I remember reading an article in a national magazine about PSS, back in 1995. The reporter had asked Cyndi Aszklar, our operations leader in New Orleans, if she thought the billion-dollar goal was achievable. "Oh, yes," Cyndi had replied. "When we say we're going to do something, we do it." And when people start believing in a goal, they make it happen.

Since we set that goal, we have branched out. PSS is now a division of a holding company known as PSS/World Medical. PSS itself remains wholly focused on serving the physician market. A new division, known as Diagnostic Imaging, serves a different part of the health-care marketplace: X-ray equipment and supplies. Our WorldMed division has expanded into Europe. Just as this book was going to press, we acquired Gulf South Medical, the largest nursing-home suppliers in the United States. We reached $1 billion in revenues in fiscal 1998, three years ahead of schedule and in half the time we thought it would take.

And sure enough, all those divisions have goals. Big, bold, ambitious goals.

PSS/World Medical seeks to be a *worldwide* distributor of medical products. There is no such company operating on a global scale today. We could be the first.

The PSS division's goal, as I write, is *to make every single employee a shareholder and have every single employee earn a bonus*. Since you can't earn a bonus unless your branch performs at a high level—see Chapter 15—this is an ambitious internal-performance goal. We want to be as good as we think we can be. We want to make sure that everybody shares in the wealth.

Diagnostic Imaging, or DI, has a five-year goal: to be a *billion-dollar* imaging distributor. Since by the end of fiscal 1998 the division had already become one of the largest sales-and-service organizations in the X-ray marketplace, I have no doubt that they will achieve their goal.

I hope you know what your company's goal is. If you don't have one, I hope you'll establish one. Knowing where you're going is the first key to building a company that can get there faster than anyone else.

Remember what I said about PSS not being unique? Years after we established PSS's initial goal of being the first national physician-supply company, I read the best-selling book Built to Last: Successful Habits of Visionary Companies, *by James C. Collins and Jerry I. Porras (HarperBusiness, 1997). Companies that are extraordinarily successful over long periods of time, say Collins and Porras, have several disinguishing characteristics. Among those characteristics is that they set what the authors dub BHAGs, for big hairy audacious goals. "A BHAG engages people—it reaches out and grabs them in the gut. It is tangible, energizing, highly focused. People 'get it' right away; it takes little or no explanation."*

I couldn't agree more. My thank-you for this chapter, though, has to go to the person I heard it from first. Thank you, Charlie Garfield.

4

A Competitive Edge

What is a business? When you get right down to it, a business is no more than people working together to deliver value to a customer. Maybe that's a cliché, but it's a cliché that no one looks at too closely. Because if they did, they'd see that it contains two indispensable keys to building a company that can leave the competition in the dust:

- *People working together.*   Obviously, it matters *how* people work together. Are they working at cross purposes, or are they cooperating effectively? Do they care about what kind of job they do? Are they learning, growing, and contributing more and more every day? This is a critically important topic, and we'll take it up in the next chapter.

- *Delivering value to the customer.*   Any company that stays in business provides something that customers are willing to pay for. But do they deliver value that the customer can't get anywhere else? That's the source of a real competitive edge—and it's what distinguishes a faster company, one that can get out front and stay there, from a company that's always jostling with a dozen competitors for a point or two of market share. This chapter tells you how to build that kind of competitive edge into the bone and muscle of your company.

Early in my career, I got a hands-on lesson about what it means to deliver value to the customer.

After graduating from Virginia Commonwealth University, I set about looking for a job. My premed training qualified me to work in the medical-products or pharmaceuticals industries. But I had a problem: Most of the fast-track jobs in those industries were in sales. You became a sales rep first. Then, if you were good enough, you moved up into management. But I wasn't interested in sales. I was shy. I didn't have much self-esteem. I didn't think I'd make a good salesperson, and I didn't really want to learn. After all, a sales rep's first job is to learn how to cope with rejection. Having been placed in the Boys Home at age five, I figured I'd had enough rejection to last a lifetime. Let somebody else do the selling!

One of the recruiters who came to the VCU campus told me, "If you're reluctant about sales, maybe you should go talk to this company, General Medical, here in Richmond." So I went over and interviewed. Sure enough, they had a management-training program that didn't seem to involve sales. I said I was interested. They hired me, and sent me down to Atlanta as a management trainee. General Medical was in the business of distributing medical products and supplies. The work was mostly in the warehouse, taking charge of stocking and inventory. That wasn't so different from what I had done as a supply sergeant in the army. I figured it was right up my alley. Later, I moved up to customer service and purchasing. I felt that I was learning a lot about operations and management.

Then one Friday afternoon, Rick Schlosser, the manager of the Atlanta branch, called me into his office. "Pat," he said, "I just had a salesman quit in Macon. I want you to go down to Macon Monday morning and start selling."

I felt a little queasy. "Rick, I didn't come to this company to sell. I want to be a manager, not a salesman."

"Pat," said Rick, "I don't think you understand. You'll go down to Macon on Monday and start selling, or you're fired."

That I could understand. Meekly, I asked, "What do I do?"

"Go to Macon and get yourself a phone book. Look in the Yellow Pages under *physicians*. I'll give you our customer list, so you'll know who's buying from us. But you call on all of them. Tell them you want their business."

Then Rick gave me a price book. And that was the extent of my sales training.

Monday morning, I showed up in Macon. If anything, the experience was even less pleasant than I had imagined it.

The guy we'd had before down there, the one who had quit, his name was Gene. Gene was a local boy. Everybody loved him. And everybody had somehow gotten the idea that General Medical had given Gene a raw deal. Every customer I called on that week, the only thing they told me was that they would *never* buy from General Medical.

And, in contrast to Gene, I was definitely not a local boy, as one customer pointed out to me in no uncertain terms.

That customer was in Dublin, Georgia, just outside of Macon. As soon as I walked into the doctor's office and introduced myself, the nurse said, "Where are you *from?* What's that accent?"

"Virginia, ma'am," I replied.

"Why, you're a *Yankee!*" she exclaimed.

"No, ma'am," I said. "I grew up in Richmond, and Richmond was the capital of the Confederacy."

That burned her up. "It was *not*. Montgomery, Alabama, was the capital of the Confederacy!"

I explained that Montgomery was the capital in the early days, but later it was moved to Richmond. (Memo to young salespeople: Don't get into debates about history with your prospects.) "I don't buy from *Yankees*," she hissed.

So nobody ordered from me. But nearly everyone I called on was glad to see me for another reason: They had something they wanted me to take back. I'd walk into a doctor's office and hear, "I don't need this any more. I want a credit from your company." Or, "I want a refund. Take this stuff back and give me a refund." That first week, it seemed like all I did was shuttle inventory back from these customers.

And at the end of the first month, I had done $14,000—in negative sales.

Rick called me in, shaking his head. "Pat," he said, "you were right. You *can't* sell. But do me a favor and stay out there until I can get a sales rep to take your place. Then we'll bring you back inside."

Well, I did go back out to Macon. And, amazingly, it got easier. I'd keep on showing up at those doctors' offices. I'd ask if they had anything on back order with one of my competitors that maybe I could get for them a little sooner. Before long I got a few orders, then a few more. My sales went from negative to positive. At the end of the fourth month, I was selling enough that Rick put me on straight commission.

I learned some of the basics of delivering value to the customer—of establishing a real competitive edge—right there in Macon, because if I didn't learn them I would have been out of a job. The more advanced lessons I learned only over time, as I moved from General Medical to Intermedco and ultimately to PSS. There are four key points.

Point 1: *Know* What the Customer Values

In Macon, the customers valued their relationship with Gene. There was nothing I could do about that; I'd have to establish my own relationship with those folks. But I quickly found out that they also valued my willingness to take things back, no questions asked. They had bought the items from Gene, not me, and maybe they couldn't find the right invoice. But it didn't matter; I'd take it back and issue them credit. Next time I stopped by I wasn't the evil outsider who had taken Gene's job, I was the kid who had taken back that stuff they didn't want.

That was my first insight into the customers I would spend my career serving. Doctors are busy. The nurses who work in their offices are busy, too. Medical supplies are low on their list of priorities, until they run out of something they need, or until some supplier sends them the wrong item. Then they want the situation corrected, and fast. They don't want to hear that you haven't got what they need. They don't want to hear that you can't deliver it until next month. They *especially* don't want to hear that the mistake isn't really your problem, it's theirs.

We built PSS around these insights.

When we started, for example, it typically took a doctor's office several days to get an order delivered by a supplier. But we were focusing exclusively on physicians' practices rather than on hospitals or nursing homes, so we didn't have any big trucks to load up. We could put their orders into one of our vans and get them out the next day. Right from the start, that was part of our guarantee: next-day service.

As we grew, some of our competitors began offering next-day service, too. So we raised the bar. We equipped our salespeople with those little laptop computers with radio transmitters attached. Then they could beam the order into the warehouse, and it would be on a truck that very afternoon. As I write, not one of our competitors can offer consistent same-day service.

What that means is simple. PSS, even though it's an ordinary, mundane business, can deliver value to the customer that no one else can.

But there's another dimension to our service that's equally important. We call it our *no-hassle guarantee*. Every order we take comes with a guarantee, spelled out on the invoice. We want you to be 100 percent satisfied with everything in this order. If there is anything at all that you're not satisfied with, we'll take it back, no questions asked. Our salespeople are taught this from day one. So are our truck drivers. Any PSS driver has the authority to take back anything, on the spot, and see that the customer gets credit. If there's any hassle at all, then we're not delivering as much value to the customer as we could be.

This is a principle that is hardly unique to PSS. Most people call it the Nordstrom principle, after the department-store chain that still sets the standard for customer service. Many other companies have adopted no-hassle service in the past decade or so. But it always amazes me how many businesses still do hassle their customers. They have policies about what they'll take back or exchange and what they won't. They make you have all the right paperwork. They make you feel like you're a real pain in the butt.

What they're doing, of course, is giving the customer a reason to buy from someone else. At PSS, we *never* want to give a customer any reason at all to buy from someone else.

Point 2: Set Up Systems to Deliver That Value Consistently

In any business, you're only as good as what you can do for the customer today. No McDonald's manager can tell a customer, "Gosh, I'm sorry that your hamburger is lousy, but remember how good yesterday's was?" And Federal Express can't say, "Gee, we really tried to get your package there overnight—and most of the time we succeed." Some of PSS's competitors offer next-day service or even same-day service when it fits into their delivery schedules. That may be an occasional convenience for a customer, but it's not a competitive edge, any more than the U.S. Postal Service has a competitive edge because a regular first-class letter occasionally reaches its destination overnight. *A competitive edge is value that you can deliver repeatedly, consistently, over and over, without fail.* It's value that customers know they can count on from you—and only from you.

So how do you build this capability? Part of the answer lies in creating systems and teaching people to use them. And part lies in a commitment that is just a little bit this side of nuts.

At PSS, for example, we couldn't provide same-day service without the laptops and the state-of-the-art computer system that serves them. But then, people need to learn the system and use it:

- Salespeople can't just call on customer after customer and write their orders up at night, as salespeople in our industry (and many other industries!) have traditionally done. They have to stop and transmit their morning orders to the warehouse, so the warehouse people can begin putting the orders on the trucks.

- Back in the warehouse, every employee has to understand the importance of world-class inventory management. We can't afford to be searching the shelves for something that is out of place. We can't afford to be out of stock on most items—and we certainly can't afford to be out of stock on an item we thought we had *in* stock.

- When the item goes out, the truck driver can't just dump it unceremoniously on the nurse's desk and hurry away; if the driver does that, we might as well have delivered it next week. So drivers have to be taught to take their time, ask the nurse where the packages should go, and help her shelve them or even unpack them. Whatever it takes to leave a customer happy with the service.

It takes time and costs money to teach people how to deliver same-day service. When we acquire a company that does things the traditional way—which is to say, virtually all of the companies we acquire—we find that it can take a year or two to get everybody up to speed on delivering same-day service.

And then there's the commitment just a little this side of nuts. If you're going to deliver something that takes this much effort, you have to be fanatical about it.

A few years back, for example, we made a decision to expand from our Houston branch into Beaumont, Texas, about 90 miles away.

Now, this was no ordinary decision. Beaumont was the headquarters location of a company called Taylor Medical. Taylor was a great company and had been one of our toughest competitors. In fact, just before we announced that PSS would be the first national physician-supply company, Taylor told the world that *they* would be the first national physician-supply company. They had raised $3 million in venture capital in 1988 to pursue this goal. We raised $2 million in 1989 and set out to beat them to it.

So we had it in for Taylor. Opening up in Beaumont meant going after them right in their own backyard, where they were making a lot of their profits.

The one thing Taylor didn't have, we knew, was same-day service. In Beaumont, as in every other city, same-day service would be one of our main competitive advantages. But every single person in that branch had to understand its importance.

Came the morning of the big day. One of our best salespeople, Todd, had been assigned to Beaumont. He hit the area at 7:00 A.M. and began calling on physicians. I happened to be visiting the Houston branch that day, and I asked to speak to the driver who would be delivering to the area.

"Todd's out selling in Beaumont this morning," I said to the driver. "He probably won't call in any orders, because he probably won't sell anything. But at eleven o'clock you are to leave with this van and drive to the city limits of Beaumont. Then you can turn around and drive back."

The driver looked at me. He said, "Yeah, sure," and walked away.

Pretty soon the branch manager called me over. "Pat," he said, "the driver says you told him to drive to Beaumont."

"That's right," I replied. "I want him to do it every day."

"But he doesn't have anything to deliver! He thinks you're crazy!"

I got the driver and the manager together, and explained two lessons I never wanted them to forget.

The first lesson was simple but important. We wanted Todd to see that van going to Beaumont every day. He'd know it was his responsibility to fill it up.

But the other lesson was even more important. We needed to have that truck going to Beaumont even if it was empty, because we *never* wanted to offer anything less than same-day service to a doctor who needed it. Suppose we hadn't sent the truck? And suppose one day the only order in Beaumont was for a single package of thermometers? Any rational manager would send the package UPS—next day—rather than put it in an otherwise empty truck. But right there, PSS's competitive edge evaporates. Suddenly we're no different from Taylor or any other competitor.

Sending out an empty truck, of course, *is* nuts. It cost us a bundle. In fact, it was four days before Todd got even one order, and several days more before he got another one. It costs a pile of money whenever we open up a new territory and start sending out trucks before our salespeople can fill them up. At PSS we always say we've shipped a lot of air from our warehouses to doctors' offices. No one pays for air, so we have to eat the cost. On the other hand, customers know that if they need something on the same day, PSS is where they'll get it. We have created a company that can deliver that extra value to the customer over and over again.

Point 3: Communicate That Value Better Than Anyone Else

This is what the rest of the world calls *selling*.

Selling has a bad reputation, even in the business world. Salespeople are seen as hucksters, con artists, and smooth talkers. They persuade you to buy something you don't really want. I think that's the view I had of selling when I started my career. I didn't feel particularly articulate, so I didn't see how I could convince anybody to buy anything.

What I learned, though, was that there's another way of looking at the sales process—an approach that accomplishes more than an army of silver-tongued sweet-talkers ever could.

What is selling, after all, but showing customers what you can do for them? And then building a relationship of trust based on the service you provide?

In Macon, the first service I had to provide was taking back the stuff people didn't want. Okay—the fact that I did that began to establish a relationship. I was someone who could provide a service. Then, I asked if they had anything on back order that maybe I could get for them sooner. Another service. Finally, I might ask for the chance to show them something that General Medical had that was maybe a little better than the competition's.

Had I been one of those individuals we call "natural" salespeople, I probably would have understood intuitively the relationship between sales and service. I was anything but a natural, so I had to learn my lessons the hard way.

When we started PSS, we wanted to build this approach to sales into the very fiber of the company. It was even reflected in our original name: Physician Sales & Service. Over time, we developed a powerful sales-training program to teach our people the approach. I'll describe that program in Chapter 8. Right now, let's just go over the basics.

Sales means communicating the services you can offer that other companies can't.   In our case, that was next-day service. Right from the start, we told people we could get them what they ordered faster than anybody else could.

Now, you might think that customers would jump at that right off the bat. But think back (if you're old enough!) to when Federal Express was brand new. Did you really have a lot of packages you wanted to send overnight? We were all accustomed to regular mail or delivery service, and we didn't know how much we would value overnight delivery. It was the same with PSS's customers. They were used to ordering in advance, and they didn't think they needed next-day, let alone same-day, service.

When they got a taste of it, though, it was different. "I can't tell you how many customers I had who would beep me," recalls Gene Dell, who is now one of our top executives but back then was a young sales rep working a territory. "And you know, when a salesperson gets a beep—'Call Dr. Jones'—your worst fear is that something has gone wrong. But it would be the nurse, and she'd be ecstatic. 'You know that stuff I ordered yesterday? I just got it today! I can't believe it!' " As people got used to next-day and, later, same-day service, they forgot how they ever got by without it.

Sales means taking the time to learn what's on customers' minds. In our industry, many of the salespeople were—and are—pure order takers. They'll go in, say hi, pick up the list of supplies that the nurse has waiting for them, and leave. But how can you communicate the services you can offer a customer if you don't know what's bothering them? Maybe the nurse or doctor is experiencing an allergic reaction to their latex gloves and needs another brand. Maybe they're worried about the cost of a particular set of supplies and would be interested in cheaper versions.

Funny thing: In this case, the services you're offering, whether it's different gloves or cheaper supplies, are services that most companies in the business can offer. But if you're the only one who takes the time to know what's on the customers' minds, you're the only one who can offer that particular service. You're communicating the value you offer better than anyone else is—just by listening.

Sales means making yourself into a valued partner of your customer. Our industry is enormously complicated. Elaborate regulations govern many of the procedures a doctor performs in the office or lab. What's more, new diagnostic equipment is coming out virtually every day. It's hard enough for a physician to keep up with new developments in medical practice, let alone with all these new regulations and equipment.

That's where our salespeople come in. They are not allowed into a territory alone until they have mastered the regulations spelled out by the Clinical Laboratory Improvement Act (CLIA) and the Occupational Safety and Health Administration (OSHA). They have learned the workings—and have been tested on their understanding—of every diagnostic machine that we sell. They attend regular seminars on the latest offerings from medical-equipment manufacturers. When they go out on the road, they're likely to know more about bone densitometry, say, or diabetes testing than most physicians. That transforms them from a salesperson in the conventional sense to a consultant, almost a partner.

We call it *consultative selling* at PSS—but what it really is is another way of communicating the value our company can offer the physicians who are our customers.

Maybe our industry is more complex than some. But these days, what business isn't complicated? And where is the company that couldn't use a little advice—real, well-informed advice—about new products or services that might solve some of its problems? And where is that advice going to come from, if not from a salesperson?

Point 4: Listen to Customers—When What They Value Changes, Change the Value You Deliver

Up until now, all these rules about delivering and communicating value have been static. But today's marketplace is nothing if not dynamic. It changes quickly and unpredictably. And a faster company has to change with it, on a dime when necessary. This is no small matter! You have to know *when* to change. You have to know *how* to change. You have to keep everyone on board while the boat is swinging around. I think it's the hardest part of creating a faster company.

We got an abrupt—not to say brutal—lesson in rapid change back in 1993.

In the first ten years of its life, PSS occupied a clearly defined niche. We offered fast, no-hassle service in our own delivery vans. For the physician's office, that meant no waiting until the hospital supplier could drop off a couple of cases of supplies. It meant no need to rely on an impersonal mail-order vendor. Our salespeople called regularly, developed a face-to-face relationship with their customers, helped solve their problems, and got them what they needed in 24 hours or less.

Naturally, all this came at a price. Our costs were higher than our competitors' costs. The prices we charged our customers were higher, too. But it didn't seem to matter: Enough physicians valued our service that we were able to grow rapidly. We were the Mercedes of our industry, and we took pride in that fact. We didn't try to compete on price, any more than Mercedes does.

Then, in 1992, Bill Clinton was elected president of the United States. And he appointed his wife, Hillary, to head up a team charged with redesigning the nation's entire health-care system.

Pretty soon, every health-care provider and institution in the country was nervous. What would the future hold? Like everyone in the industry, PSS's salespeople were talking about the current environment with the doctors and nurses who were their customers. But amidst all the general handwringing, they never picked up on a specific development, a development that could have jeopardized the future of PSS.

Fortunately, we had a secret source of information.

Every six months or so, we survey our customers. It's done through an outside firm, so they don't know it's PSS that's asking the questions and they're more likely to give us the unvarnished truth. We try to reach a broad sample, usually about 1,000. But we keep it simple. We ask our customers, for example, what they value most in a medical-products distributor. We ask them to rank three factors: their relationship with the sales representative, the service they get from the distributor, and the prices they have to pay.

In the past, the answers from our survey had always been crystal clear. Relationship was number one by a wide margin, service was a comfortable second, and price was dead last. Typically, only about 12 percent of customers told the interviewer that they made buying decisions primarily based on price. If we ever had doubts about our Mercedes strategy, the survey boosted our confidence that we were doing the right thing.

Until 1993. That year, the survey turned upside down.

It was February, right after Clinton's inauguration. Doctors were hearing from Washington that they were making too much money. They were hearing that managed care was coming, and that they would have to learn to be cost-effective. Not to put too fine a point on it, they were panicking. When the survey came back, price had jumped to the top of their concerns. Now, about 70 percent were saying that price was the chief factor influencing their decision. Service was still second—and relationship with the sales rep was dead last.

In effect, customers were going into a very aggressive shopping mode. They weren't looking to buy a Mercedes any more, they wanted a Chevrolet. And those sales reps that they were so fond of? If the reps couldn't give them cheap product, those reps were history.

PSS had to change. We had to change fast, and we had to change dramatically.

Fortunately, we had some things going for us as we considered our options. We were coming up on the end of our fiscal year, so it was a good time to make a move. We were still privately held, so we didn't have Wall Street looking over our shoulder and second-guessing us. We had become one of the largest players in the marketplace, so we had some clout with our suppliers. Right away, we lowered our own pricing 20 percent on our top 100 items. We consolidated product lines and negotiated price breaks from the vendors we kept. We began offering a line of low-cost private-label products. We established a buying club that promised physicians steep price breaks if they bought most of their supplies from us.

Easy, right? Sure. Except that most of our people thought the other executives and I had gone *really* nuts—as in stark, raving mad.

You could hardly blame them. We were the ones who had preached for ten years that PSS was the Mercedes of the industry. We were the ones who had told the salespeople, don't apologize for higher prices, just show customers the extra value we deliver. We were the ones who said, what physicians and nurses really value are their relationships with you, the sales reps.

Now we were saying the exact opposite. Worse still, we were threatening their incomes. Commissioned salespeople like price cuts about as much as politicians like term limits. And they howled. As John Sasen, who was then the chief operating officer of PSS, put it, "There were three months of what I'd have to call paralysis in the organization."

Well, we went on the road. We spent those three months talking with people in every single branch. I gave my annual soapbox speech at the national sales meeting and explained to everybody why we were doing what we were doing.

The logic of our move was hard to ignore. Slowly, the salespeople came around. In fact, not one left the company, even though competitors were wooing the best of them all the time.

Slowly, too, PSS began to realize the benefits of the new strategy. Sure, we took a hit in our margins. But we also began filling up our vans. Instead of delivering the one or two small packages that the customer bought from us, we were delivering large quantities of product—which meant that our overhead costs as a percent of sales came down. Overall, we were learning to squeeze costs out of our system, even while we maintained our high level of service. None of our salespeople got hurt in the pocketbook, and before long most of them had learned how to communicate the new value that PSS could deliver. Soon their incomes were even higher than they had been before the change. The customer was buying more product from PSS reps and was more dependent than ever on the value those reps could provide.

Looking back on this experience, I draw three conclusions.

First, this was a particularly dramatic example of how the marketplace can change on you in a heartbeat. Health care has been an unusually volatile industry in the last few years. But again: How many industries aren't changing fast? Consumers and business buyers don't have much brand loyalty any more. If you think you can build a company around delivering only one kind of value to a customer—if you think you'll never have to change— you're making a big mistake. You have to listen to the customer *very* carefully.

Second, often what you learn from listening to the customer isn't one big thing, it's a lot of little things. That episode in 1993 is the only time, so far, that we've had to redirect our whole strategy. But just recently, we began surveying our customers about what they liked and disliked in their dealings with PSS. One thing they told us was that our invoicing system wasn't providing all the information they wanted. We went to work on that right away.

Finally, the task you face in building a faster company isn't just knowing when to change, it's creating a company that *can* change. Most companies can't. This brings us to the other part of the business equation: people working together. We'll get to that in the next chapter.

In the meantime, think back on the four elements of a real competitive edge. You know what the customer values. You set up systems that can deliver that value consistently, day in and day out, in ways that the competition can't. You communicate what you can provide to the customer through the sales process. And you listen to customers, so that when what they value changes, you can change with them.

Once you understand these principles, you can put them into practice in nearly any business.

In 1995, for example, we reached our goal of becoming the first national physician-supply company. (The key step? The day we bought Taylor Medical, the company that we had attacked in Beaumont. That gave us national reach in one fell swoop.) We would continue to grow in this marketplace. But we also began looking for another segment of the health-care market in which we could replicate the kind of explosive growth—hypergrowth—that we had experienced in PSS.

In 1996, we found it: X-ray supply distribution. The 200 or so companies that sold radiology supplies and serviced X-ray machines were mostly local and regional operations. We figured we could acquire them and add value, based on the PSS model.

We made our first acquisition in November 1996. Today, our Diagnostic Imaging division is one of the largest providers of X-ray supplies and equipment to hospitals and physicians. Value to the customer? What's important in this industry is different from what's important in the physician-supply market. There aren't so many different kinds of supplies, for example, and supplies are consumed more slowly. Next-day or same-day service isn't so critical. What *is* critical is what happens when an X-ray machine breaks down. Until that machine is back up and running, the facility is out of operation.

So here's what DI offers: any time a customer calls with a breakdown, we will respond by telephone within 30 minutes. And we'll have someone on the spot to begin repairs within two hours—any time of day, anywhere in our service area. Nobody else in the business is set up to deliver that kind of value. We have organized our company around it, and we make sure our salespeople communicate it to the customer. In every other respect, DI is built on the PSS model. Like PSS, for example, the DI division has a goal: to be a billion-dollar company in five years.

Then there's our brand-new nursing-home division. One factor that made Gulf South Medical such an attractive acquisition candidate is that they are the low-cost supplier. This is a market in which government reimbursement schedules determine most prices, so the low-cost supplier has a natural competitive advantage. Gulf South Medical had it, and we intend to keep it.

Maybe someday these markets will change the way the physicians market did in 1993. If so, we hope we can change with them. If we do, we will surely reach our goal. That's what a competitive edge—a real competitive edge—can do for you.

Thank you, Fred Smith. Plenty of companies have been built around unique capabilities, but in my view no one had quite the vision of the man who created Federal Express. Smith not only decided there was a market for overnight delivery, he was willing to bet the farm on it. He had to line up airplanes before he had any packages to ship. He had to create a retrieval, sorting, and delivery system of a kind that no one had ever seen before. When he expanded into new markets—Asia, for example—he had to fly a lot of nearly empty planes until demand could catch up with supply. It was a bold, risky, creative, and immensely rewarding strategy for company building, one that we're proud to have learned from at PSS.

A Company of CEOs

Here's how people work together in conventional companies: They all do their jobs.

Executives plot strategies. Managers manage. Employees do as they're told. How people work together is governed by job descriptions, lines of authority, rules and regulations, and all the other trappings of hierarchy and bureaucracy. Ever heard the phrase, "Hey, that's not *my* job" from someone in your organization? The fact is, given the way most businesses are organized, that's a perfectly legitimate response to many requests. People are told exactly what their job is. They're told to *do it* without thinking about it. You can't really blame them for not wanting to do someone else's job.

At standout companies—faster companies—the situation is a little different. People do what needs to be done. They pitch in.

They *want* the company to succeed, and they do everything they can to help it along.

The PSS phrase that describes this attitude is *a company of CEOs*. We tell our people to think and act as if they're all chief executive officers. We put CEO on truck drivers' business cards. We got hats made up that read CEO, and we passed them out. We literally want everyone to see himself or herself as top dog in the company.

Now, I get a lot of weird looks when I talk to business audiences about all these CEOs.

Most people seem to figure it's just another hokey PSS notion that nobody takes too seriously. After all, we do have a *real* chief executive officer. And we do run a regular business, with salespeople and truck drivers and accountants and customer-service reps. Not everybody is sitting in a corner office plotting strategies and talking to Wall Street analysts.

But the fact is, we take the notion of every man and woman a CEO very, very seriously. It's an idea that completely redefines how people in an organization work together. It has a series of specific implications for how you structure the business. Ultimately, it's what allows a company such as PSS to perform at a higher level—a level that competitors can't match.

In this chapter I'll spell out exactly what the idea means to us. First, though, I want to tell you a little about where it came from. It's strange. It was my experience in what may be the most bureaucratic, hierarchical organization around that convinced me that everybody *can* be a CEO.

Any healthy young man who flunked out of college in the late 1960s, as I did, didn't have much of a choice about his immediate future. The U.S. armed forces would be glad to decide his future for him. My draft notice arrived soon after I left Virginia Commonwealth University. I showed up at a big gym in Richmond for my induction. There were about 300 of us there. A sergeant got up on the podium and began to speak.

"All you boys here were drafted," he began. "So let me tell you what's going to happen to you."

We milled around nervously, but we listened.

"You know there's a war on, over in a place called Vietnam. Since all of you were drafted, you're gonna wind up in the infantry. You'll be going to Vietnam just as soon as we can get you there. And the chances are real good that you'll all be killed."

Now he definitely had our attention.

"It so happens that there are some positions open in the supply corps. You'll have to sign up for an additional year if you want to get into supply. But if you do, you won't have to go in the infantry."

Then he got to the punch line. "Okay. All those interested in supply, please move to the right-hand side of the gym."

Within minutes, 297 of the 300 young men in the room had moved to the right-hand side of the gym. I never did find out what happened to the other three, but my own immediate future was clear as day. I would be in supply. I'd also be in the army an extra year. Compared to the alternative the sergeant was promising, that didn't seem so bad.

As a matter of fact, it wasn't so bad—for a while.

After my basic training, the army offered me a chance to attend Officer Candidate School. At first I liked the idea, so I went to Fort Lee, Virginia, and waited to rotate into OCS. They made me an acting platoon sergeant and put me in charge of teaching calisthenics. By the time I had to actually sign up for OCS, though, I had changed my mind. I knew I didn't want to make a career in the army. Nor did I want to enlist for yet another extra year, which OCS would require.

So I'd stay in supply. But even when I got the orders sending me to Vietnam, it didn't seem so bad. My destination was in Saigon. At the time, Saigon was far from the front lines. I arrived in country in early January, 1968, and wrote my wife, Judy, a letter as soon as I got off the airplane. Don't worry about me, I said. There won't be any fighting here.

I hadn't heard the words *Tet Offensive*, of course. Nobody else had either—because January 1968 marked the beginning of the Tet offensive. The very night I arrived in country, at 2:00 A.M., a prelude to the offensive was launched. My compound in Saigon came under sudden and unexpected attack.

It was a night of sheer terror. Mortar shells were falling all around. Enemy soldiers were coming at us. U.S. Marines were doing their best to defend the camp, but the numbers were against them. We new guys hadn't even been issued weapons. Suddenly we got the word: Get yourselves to the Thai transport ship down at the dock. Quick! We left our bags and equipment at the compound and ran on board ship. In less than 30 minutes that ship was out of there. Just before the camp was overrun, we managed to escape down the river and get out to the South China Sea.

We sat out there on the South China Sea for three weeks, incommunicado. We ate C rations that they helicoptered out to us. We lounged around on deck, waiting. Judy, of course, had been watching television and hearing about how Saigon was being overrun. She hadn't heard a word from me—and then she got my letter telling her I would be in Saigon and not to worry. For a good two weeks she thought I was dead. It wasn't until they finally landed us at Da Nang that I could call her to let her know I wasn't.

I'll never forget the night we landed in Da Nang, either, and not just because I finally got to call Judy.

It was January 31, my twenty-first birthday and the Tet new year. The offensive had already spread north to Da Nang. The people who ran our camp suspected there would be an attack that night. We were supply, not infantry, but they pressed us into service to defend the perimeter of the camp. A sergeant called us all together and asked us: "Who here knows how to fire an M-60?"

An M-60 was a machine gun. We had no idea. Nobody raised a hand.

The sergeant wouldn't be stopped. "Okay, who here has ever been in a leadership role?"

We were all privates first class. But without thinking, I raised my hand. "I was waiting for OCS, and they made me an acting platoon sergeant at Fort Lee for three months."

"Great," said the sergeant. "You'll man the M-60." He didn't want to hear my protests that I didn't know how to fire it. "You were officer candidate material," he said, putting an end to the conversation. "You'll figure it out."

It takes three men to handle an M-60, so I was assigned two helpers. These guys were carrying ammo boxes, and now they were all excited. Maybe they had seen too many war movies, because they had this idea that they could mow down the enemy with our one M-60. I had seen some war movies myself, but I had come away with the opposite lesson: I knew that the enemy would come after the machine gunners first. When I conveyed my understanding of our situation to them, they got a little less excited.

Somehow, we figured out how to fire the M-60. Fortunately for us, though, the attack came not by sea, where the three of us were stationed, but by land. Fortunately, too, that night wasn't a replay of what happened. Our soldiers were prepared this time. They beat back the enemy handily. The U.S. army maintained control of that camp for the 11 months that I remained in country after that. Once in a while we'd undergo a mortar attack—the Viet Cong seemed to have a knack for blowing up our outhouses with their mortars—but the camp was never in danger of being overrun.

The point of this brief Vietnam memoir isn't to make me out to be a war hero, which I wasn't. I was just an ordinary grunt doing the job he was assigned to do. But it was that experience more than anything else that I took back with me when my stint in the service was over and that affected my thinking about people and organizations.

Think about it. An army in wartime doesn't have a lot of choice about its personnel. They come from all walks of life. They may not have much education. Nearly all of them are young—some are barely out of high school—and many of them would dearly love to be somewhere else doing something completely different. In short, it's an organization that should be able to accomplish nothing.

And yet: Armies accomplish amazing things.

Even in Vietnam. Granted, Vietnam wasn't exactly a high point in U.S. military history. But if you were there, you saw strategies carried out, victories won, huge numbers of men and huge amounts of equipment deployed. I think armies can accomplish what they do mostly because individuals rise to the occasion. They perform at a level they didn't know they were capable of.

That was sure true for me. There I was, age 21. I had been a C student in high school. I had flunked out of college. I had gotten a little training in the service, but I never did go to Officer Candidate School. In Vietnam, however, the army assigned me responsibility for issuing every last one of the vehicles going to the northern part of South Vietnam. At that time the United States had about 30,000 vehicles in country—jeeps, tanks, half-ton trucks, and so on—and every vehicle going into northern South Vietnam had to go through me. At home, I was barely old enough to buy a beer. In Vietnam, at war, I was responsible for hundreds of millions of dollars' worth of equipment.

What's more, this was real responsibility. I wasn't just carrying out someone else's orders. Plenty of times I had to figure out how to get a vehicle to a marine corporal whose jeep had just been blown out from under him. Usually that meant some colonel or general didn't get the jeep he was expecting. The brass would yell at me, then they'd yell at my lieutenant. But my lieutenant was a man who believed in delegating, and he'd back me to the hilt. As far as he was concerned, the decisions were mine to make. And so they were.

I was hardly alone in having so much responsibility. Quite the contrary: The army was famous for it. *Give people responsibility and we'll see what they can do.* As it turns out, most people can do a helluva lot. Ask them to accomplish something, and more often than not they'll accomplish it—even if they are still wet behind the ears.

Of course, once this particular cat is out of the bag, the brass have to live with the initiatives their empowered front-line people take.

At Da Nang, it wasn't bad enough that we had to keep rebuilding our outhouses after they were hit by enemy mortar fire. We also had no hot water for showers. At one point, I realized I might be in a position to do something about this. A group of navy Seabees—construction battalions—approached me. They needed some vehicles and couldn't get them through the navy. I said they'd have to repaint them, green to gray, but they didn't care. Besides, they said, maybe we could use a hot-water heater. They had one in Okinawa. If I got them the vehicles, they'd see that the hot-water heater was flown in. They'd even hook it up for us.

It sounded good to me. I got them two three-quarter-ton trucks and sat back to wait for the hot-water heater.

Alas, my lieutenant found out what I was up to. And that was the one time he didn't back me up. Matter of fact, he and the other officers got together and confiscated the hot-water heater and hooked it up themselves, for officers only. We enlisted men were still taking cold showers. It wasn't for another few months that I was able to track down a hot-water heater in San Antonio and swap a jeep to people who could get it for us. Even then, we were the first GIs in the north to have hot showers.

So rank does have its privileges, and the brass won't always give you the authority you think you deserve. But that wasn't the real lesson I took back from my days in Vietnam.

I went to Vietnam young and untested. Like most soldiers—those lucky enough to come home alive—I returned as an adult. Before, I didn't have much self-esteem. After, I knew what I could do. I could get things done, make things happen. But it wasn't me, it was the situation I had been put in. The army had encouraged me to learn and take responsibility. They had trusted me to do what needed to be done, and had backed me up (at least most of the time). They had assumed that *I was capable of thinking for myself and making decisions with the army's best interests at heart.*

That's what we at PSS mean by saying that our people are CEOs. We've tried to build a company that makes it possible for them—that encourages them—to think and act as if they were in charge, to make decisions with the company's best interests at heart.

A company of CEOs, of course, is bound to look different from a conventional business in just about every way you can imagine. It's going to be structured differently. The expectations will be different. There won't be the same lines of authority. The way people are paid won't be the same. If you want to build a faster company, in fact, you'll have to gather up most of the principles people take for granted about how an organization should work, then throw them out the window.

And what goes in their place? Really, it's just four simple ideas.

Idea 1: Run an *Open* Company

Most companies are dens of secrecy. One department doesn't know what another is doing. Information is distributed on a need-to-know basis. Memos are confidential. Nobody sees the numbers. You've probably worked in organizations like this, and it's no wonder that the people in them do only what they're asked to do. If they tried to do anything else, they wouldn't know where to begin. Then, too, they have to figure they're not trusted. Why should they put themselves out for an organization that has no faith in them?

At PSS, it's different. Everything is open.

The numbers, for example. We're firm believers in the philosophy known as *open-book management*. Every branch has its goals, and everyone in the branch knows what they are. Branch leaders distribute P&Ls at monthly meetings and are charged with making sure people understand those numbers. Most of the branches post performance numbers—including performance numbers for individual salespeople, since those numbers drive the branch's income statement—right up on the wall where people can inspect them. As for the salespeople, they have all the information about our business literally at their fingertips, on those laptop computers that they take wherever they go.

To me, open-book is just common sense. Most companies today are open-book whether they want to be or not, just because people are pretty good at finding out information they're interested in. It's getting harder and harder for any organization to keep secrets. We figure: Why try?

The open culture at PSS goes beyond regular sharing of the financials. The other leaders and I tell people when we visit a branch that they can ask us anything they want. Unless we're bound by a legal confidentiality agreement, we'll answer it. How much money do we make? What are PSS's gross margins on a given product line? Where are we looking to expand next? A while ago we started a practice of passing out $2 bills to people who ask questions, just to help them get over any nervousness they may feel about sounding stupid. Now we're probably the biggest users of $2 bills in northern Florida. People at PSS ask a *lot* of questions. And not just of me: They'll ask questions of their branch leaders, their regional vice presidents, and people visiting from another facility. Everyone knows the rule: No question is off limits. Every question not covered by a confidentiality agreement needs an answer.

(Sometimes we're asked how much is covered by those confidentiality agreements. The fact is, not a whole lot. We have some confidential arrangements with manufacturers. Since we went public, we can release our consolidated financials to employees only at the same time we release them to the public. It's ironic: When we were privately held, we could be even more open than we are now. Still, what matters most to our employees is the performance of their own branch. That's what they can affect directly, and that's what determines their bonuses.)

One more symbol of openness is important: open doors. At PSS, we *hate* closed doors.

When some people are talking behind closed doors, other people get nervous. What's being discussed? Are they talking about me? Is there something I'm not supposed to know? You can walk into PSS's corporate headquarters or any of PSS's branches, and I'll challenge you to find a closed door other than the one on the bathroom.

And if you do find one, I can guarantee you it won't be there long. Literally. Not so long ago, for example, our Diagnostic Imaging division acquired a company in North Carolina. Gene Dell, who runs DI, explained our open-door philosophy to the managers there. He heard back that there were still some closed-door meetings going on, so he explained it again. The third time, he figured he had to make the point a little more forcefully. Today, there are *no* doors on the offices of that branch.

It's the same at the executive offices. When people come to our offices they need to know they can walk into any office on the executive level, the CEO's included, and talk to the person in that office. We don't want *anybody* waiting outside because a door is shut.

Idea 2: Give People Authority—and Accountability

People who have easy access to information are one step of the way toward thinking of themselves as CEOs. They know that nobody's holding back on them. They know that the company trusts them with all possible information about the business. The next step is knowing that they have the authority to act on the information.

You have the authority. This is something we tell our people over and over. It's the main reason we put CEO on those hats and business cards. When you're standing in front of the customer, you *are* the CEO. You have the power to do whatever it takes to satisfy the customer. As Jan Carlzon of SAS Airlines put it in his book, every interaction with a customer is a moment of truth that determines what the customer will think of your company. Sometimes a truck driver or customer-service rep might need more information before making a decision. That's fine. But it's his or her job to get that information right away and then to take action. If they're thinking like a CEO, they'll always do what's right for the customer. Should I send a truck on a special trip out to that office? Should I fix this doctor's table right here and now? Well, what would you expect if you were the customer?

I wish I could magically communicate this principle to all of our people, because it can take a while to sink in.

Not long ago, for example, we bought a company in Knoxville, Tennessee. Soon after the acquisition, I went up to visit the branch and invited the salespeople out to dinner. We went to a local rib joint called Calhoun's. A group of salespeople is usually a lively bunch, and we were having a good time.

At one point, though, I noticed that a salesman named Chris was down in the mouth. He was at the other end of the table from me. He wasn't taking part in any of the joking and talking. He looked as if he wanted to be somewhere else. *Anywhere* else.

I got up and went around to talk to him. "Hey, Chris," I said, "what's the matter? Aren't things working out for you?"

He gave me a doleful look. "You don't know what happened yesterday?" I shook my head and asked what happened. He looked even more dejected. "You're going to fire me when you find out."

"Chris," I said, "I'm not going to fire you. Tell me what happened."

Slowly, the story came out. Chris was selling maybe $40,000 a month at that time. Then he had suddenly hit it big: He sold a doctor in nearby Cleveland, Tennessee, a complete laboratory setup. Chris had been ecstatic—until just the day before our dinner, when the doctor had told him he wanted to send the whole thing back. "I said I *would* take it back, the doctor hadn't yet used any of the equipment. I hope you don't fire me."

I burst out laughing. "Fire you?" I exclaimed. "I want to kiss you!" And I explained that was exactly what we expected of PSS people. He had made a decision on the spot, with the best interests of the customer in mind. That doctor undoubtedly knew all the other doctors in Cleveland. He'd tell them how the PSS rep had treated him. Now, there's a company a physician would want to do business with. Long term, Chris and PSS would *own* that town.

The other side of authority, of course, is accountability. People at PSS take responsibility for their decisions.

Most companies get this exactly backward: They expect their people to be accountable, but they don't give them much authority. We expect people to assume authority *and* accountability.

Most companies get something else backward, too. They think that holding people accountable means punishing them for their mistakes. This was the kind of thinking Chris was expecting.

Well, Chris hadn't made a mistake. But what if he had? People do. And the more decisions you expect them to make, the more often they'll screw up. In fact, if they aren't making mistakes, they probably aren't making decisions.

We have another saying at PSS: *It's easier to ask for forgiveness than permission.* Go ahead and make a decision. If you make the wrong one, acknowledge your mistake and learn from it. Then move on. Nobody at PSS will punish you. (However, we hope our people don't make the same mistake twice!)

Idea 3: Share the Wealth

A successful business creates enormous amounts of wealth. And in most companies, who gets it? Shareholders, of course. The chief executive. Other senior managers. Sometimes the top salespeople will make a lot of money—except that the best of them will usually max out, which is to say that they'll hit the cap the company places on their incomes. After all, you can't have salespeople making more than the CEO, can you?

As for everybody else, they'll get the wages or salary that the market determines, and maybe a small bonus at Christmastime.

PSS works a little differently. Yes, we pay market-based wages and salaries. They're toward the high end in most local markets, but they're still market rates. Yes, a leader earns more than an employee. A vice president makes more than someone in the warehouse.

But we believe that everybody helps create the wealth at PSS and that everybody should share in it. We do our best to make sure that every employee owns stock. Our employee stock-ownership plan (ESOP) is PSS's biggest single shareholder. We also pay fat bonuses to successful branches, and everybody in the branch gets an equal share (see Chapter 15). You may be a truck driver making $20,000 a year, but if your branch is a high performer you could get an additional $6,000 or $8,000 in bonuses.

One more thing: We never, ever put a cap on what commissioned salespeople can earn. Why would we? We don't really care if a salesperson earns more than a regional vice president. We don't care if he or she makes more than the CEO. We want the very best salespeople we can find, and we want to reward them for every dollar's worth of value they provide our customers. If they wind up earning $200,000 in a year, good for them.

Idea 4: Have Leaders, Not Managers

Funny thing about a company of CEOs. People who think of themselves as CEOs don't really want to be told what to do.

In the past, that was more or less a manager's job: Tell people what to do. It still is at many companies. At PSS, we expect people to figure out for themselves what to do.

When I get to this point in a speech about building a company of CEOs, you can feel the skepticism in the audience. *Oh, sure. Let everybody figure out what to do. Might as well put the monkeys in charge of the zoo.*

But stop and think for a minute, because how we do things really isn't so hard to understand.

First, all our people have jobs. They're hired as salespeople or truck drivers or customer-service reps. We haven't abolished the division of labor, so they understand where their primary responsibility lies. And, as you'll see in Chapter 8, they get plenty of training.

Second, they know the branch's goals, and they learn to understand the numbers that measure progress toward those goals. They can see month by month how they're doing on gross revenue and gross margin, how close expenses are to plan, and where the problem areas and new opportunities might be.

Third, they have a reason to care. They're shareholders in the company. They get bonuses only if their branch meets its performance targets.

Fourth, they can get all the help and coaching they want from the branch's leaders.

Put all those factors together, and you get people who *can* think and act like CEOs. They may have different jobs. They may be on salary or on commission or on an hourly wage. But nobody can tell me that they're employees, at least not in the ordinary sense. I've seen employees at other companies I've worked for and visited. Employees do as they're told. Employees really don't care how the company they work for performs. Employees do their jobs, pick up their checks, and go home. PSS has no employees, only CEOs.

We also don't have any managers. Managers, as I said, tell people what to do, and people at PSS don't need to be told what to do. What do they need? They need leadership. They need inspiration and guidance. They need advice and teaching. They need help when a particularly tough problem comes along. A leader at PSS is expected to provide all that.

We practice what Gandhi preached—namely, that *a true leader is the servant of the people he or she leads*. Wiser words were never spoken.

Make no mistake, however: This is not some soft, muddle-headed approach. PSS isn't a social club, it's a business with clear objectives. We intend to meet those objectives month in and month out. The job of a leader, whether branch leader or regional vice president or chief executive, is to help his or her people meet their goals. If goals aren't met, it's a sign that someone needs help, and we devote all the resources we can to providing that help. If goals aren't met repeatedly, it's a sign that someone's in the wrong job. At that point we'll take steps to correct the situation, usually by changing leaders. After all, not everybody is cut out to be a leader. At PSS, it's no crime to fail at leadership, it's just a sign that you need to be in another job.

What *is* a crime is how so many businesses, even today, still think they can manage people. They can't. You have to give people direction, and point them where you want them to go. You have to set the parameters, and coach them along the way. You have to give them responsibility and offer them rewards commensurate with their performance.

Then you have to get the hell out of the way.

———

There's a reason, of course, for creating a company of CEOs. That's what enables you to do things your competitors can't do.

It's possible that even a casual visitor to our branches would notice the difference between PSS and more ordinary businesses. Our trucks are spiffy. Our drivers are dressed in clean, pressed uniforms. Nobody in the warehouse is lounging around. The facility itself is attractive, the bathrooms sparkling, the desks neat. When the phone rings, chances are good it'll be picked up immediately. If it should ring again, people will be diving across desks to answer it. Everybody at a PSS branch understands a basic truth about business, which is that a company that doesn't do little things well won't be able to do big things well. How can we expect customers to trust us with their orders if we can't run a tight, shipshape operation—including answering the phone on the first or second ring?

But the real payoff from creating this kind of company comes only over time. And most of it takes place behind the scenes.

Exceptional Performance

CEOs work long hours and do extraordinary things for the good of their company. Every year we recognize some of our people who have done just that. PSSers, we say, don't grow on trees. So we hand out dozens of Don't Grow on Trees Awards to people who have gone the extra mile to take care of a customer, just as any CEO would.

Examples? Here are a couple. During the 1997 United Parcel Service strike, some of our drivers crossed picket lines to pick up packages stuck in a UPS depot—packages our customers needed. Employees often come in late at night to our warehouse so they can get product to physicians' offices in time for early-morning surgery. Or maybe they'll drive a couple hours out of their way on the way home, just so the doctor gets product that day rather than the next.

Continuous Improvement

Then there are the kinds of small initiatives that nobody sees, but that make a huge difference to a company's performance over time. I think, for instance, of our accounts-payable department in the corporate offices.

Back when we were doing $20 million in sales, we had three employees in payables. As I write, we're coming up on our first billion-dollar year, so we probably should have at least 30 people in the department. Instead, we have ten. And I don't think anybody could say we're pushing these employees too hard. PSS is based in a region with low unemployment. An experienced accounts-payable clerk would have no trouble finding a job. But we have had very little turnover in this department.

How do we improve productivity like this? Well, *we* don't. *They* do. The people in payables take responsibility for figuring out how to do their job better every year.

One thing they did, for example, was to begin staggering their hours. Some come in at six o'clock in the morning and leave at two in the afternoon. Others come in at ten and go home at six. They get more done, they say, during those early-morning and late-afternoon hours than during regular business hours—but there's still always someone there from nine to five to answer the phone.

Occasionally, they'd come to me or to one of the other executives and ask for a new person. Sometimes we'd agree that they needed one. More often, we'd offer them another deal: If they could figure out how to get the work done without adding an employee, we'd take half the salary that new person would have earned and divide it among the existing employees in payables. The way it seems to work out is, every other year they really do have to add one more body. In the intervening years, they figure out how to get the work done without any more people.

A couple of years ago, they felt they could actually eliminate a position by changing the way we filed our invoices. Basically, it came down to introducing a batch filing system, which they said would eliminate 90 percent of the time they spent filing invoices. We set up a test. We had some people from Arthur Andersen come in and see if they could find the new invoices as fast under the new system as under the old. It worked like a charm. We were actually able to take one person out of payables and find a job for her elsewhere in the company.

I know that many, many companies have spent a lot of time and money hiring consultants and introducing formal quality and continuous-improvement programs. I don't have anything against those programs, but I recommend an alternative: Create a company of CEOs who think and work on improvements all the time.

Loyalty and Commitment

Remember that story in the previous chapter about how we had to turn on a dime in 1993? When we cut our prices, most of our salespeople weren't happy. They knew they'd take a hit in their commissions. But none of them left. They knew why we were making the moves we did. They knew they would benefit in the long run if the moves were successful.

That wasn't the only time we asked our employees to make a sacrifice. In 1991, we were having a tough year. It was the time of the Gulf War. We were expanding at breakneck speed, including setting up operations in Texas. It looked that year as if we would lose money. If we did, we would be in violation of our covenants with the bank, and we'd probably get our credit line pulled. We never wanted to give a bank an excuse to bounce us, because we were always getting bounced anyway. Finally, we didn't see any alternative: Since 55 percent of every dollar we spend as a company goes into payroll, we had to ask everyone to take a pay cut. It would start at the top. The other executives and

I would give up 20 percent of our salaries. Truck drivers and warehouse workers would be asked to give up 3 percent of theirs.

At the time, PSS had more than 500 employees. The cuts lasted for four months. The number of people who left during that time was negligible.

CEOs don't quit when the going gets tough. They stick around, pitch in, work harder. And they know they'll be rewarded if they can get the company back on track. When we got back on track, we made up all that lost pay.

Thank you, Jan Carlzon. Carlzon's book, Moments of Truth *(Harper Collins, 1989), helped us understand that we wanted to build a company in which everyone could deal with customers, solve problems, and make decisions just as if they were all CEOs. That, says Carlzon, is the way it works at SAS, the Scandinavian airline. And that's the way it works at PSS.*

CHAPTER 6

Values

Let's look back at the other three chapters in this section on the building blocks of a faster company. The first one—Chapter 3—focuses on setting ambitious goals. Chapter 4 is about establishing a competitive edge, which is another way of saying taking care of the customer better than anybody else. Chapter 5 is about creating a company of CEOs—an organization that makes it possible for everybody to perform at a high level. Since we at PSS stole all our good ideas, you'll find echoes of these lessons in a lot of business books and case studies. Federal Express has that competitive edge. SAS Airlines—and here at home, Southwest Airlines—expect their people to think and act like CEOs.

This chapter, however, is about a subject most businesspeople don't like to talk much about. It's about values. It's about how you treat people, why you do the things you do, and how you create an organization that embodies what you believe is right.

I'm not sure why businesspeople don't like to talk about values. Maybe they think that a company's only purpose is to make money.

But companies aren't in business only to make money. Money is important, sure. A company needs money to survive. People invest in a business in hopes of earning a return. They go to work every day in hopes of making a good living. But money to a company is like food and water to a human being. You need a certain amount just to survive. You need more if you want to grow and stay healthy. But once you have what you need, getting more is rarely your only purpose in life.

In thinking about values, it helps to go back to that definition of business we came up with earlier. *A business is people working together to deliver value to a customer.* Surely it matters *how* we work together and *what* we provide our customers with. Would you really want to be part of an organization in which people snarled at each other, didn't trust one another, or browbeat their subordinates? Would you feel good about working for a company that tried to cheat its customers with defective goods or inadequate service? To me, achieving business goals is great. But no business goal is worth sacrificing your values. If you have to treat people poorly or cut corners in your dealings with customers, forget it.

The fact is, most of us spend more hours working than we spend at any other single activity. We spend more time at the workplace than anywhere else. If values aren't important in business, where are they are important?

Growing up, most of us get our values from sources close to home. From our parents and from other family members and friends. From teachers, coaches, and religious leaders. From authors and others who speak to us through the media. Maybe you can remember one or two people who had a powerful influence on your own values.

I certainly can. Some of the values that we try to build into PSS today are values that I learned at an early age, in the Virginia Home for Boys.

I don't remember much before I turned five and went to live in the Home. I think I must have been well taken care of, by my aunts and my sister and my mother when she was able. But it was a tough situation. When my father left, my mother didn't have any money. She was too proud to accept help from her family, so she worked long hours and had to rely on others to take care of my brother and me. Finally, she persuaded the Home to accept both of us even though I was so young.

I do remember the day she took us to the Home. I was scared to death. My early experiences there didn't do much to allay my fears. The older boys used me as a punching bag until I learned to fight back by sinking my teeth into them. But the problems a kid faces in that situation are psychological more than physical. At age five, I really didn't know why I had been put in the Home. Like most of the Home's boys, then and now, I figured there must be something wrong with me.

Still, it's interesting to think back on life at the Home. It wasn't the kind of grim, dreary orphanage you might picture.

We lived in cottages. The cottages all had housemothers— warm, kindly women who did their best to take care of us. Mrs. Moore and Mrs. James, two of the housemothers in my cottages, lavished attention on me, since I was the youngest kid there. We had a lot of fun. We were close to Byrd Park in Richmond. On weekends, we'd get grocery boxes and slide down the grass hills. There was a lake in the park where we could swim. Of course, we didn't have a whole lot of time for playing. We grew our own vegetables on adjacent farmland: corn, potatoes, lettuce, and turnips. We had to get up early, do our household chores, go to school, then come back and work in the fields.

So the Home taught us all the value of hard work. But living there also instilled in us some lessons, both good and bad, about how to treat people. Three experiences stand out in my mind.

The first one occurred when I was about eight.

I was given a model airplane for Christmas, and I wanted to build it. Trouble was, I didn't have any glue. Our allowance at that point was a nickel a week, and I had spent my nickel on the movies. But I *really* wanted to put that airplane together.

So I walked down Cary Street and into Rose's 5 & 10. I found the glue and picked out a tube. Then I looked around, stuck the tube in my pocket, and made for the door.

They grabbed me just as I was walking out the door. It turned out they had been watching me the whole time. After all, wasn't I one of those kids from the Home? They took me to the back of the store and called the police. When the police came, I tried not to tell them I was from the Home, because I was terrified about what might happen to me. But I finally broke down and admitted it, yes, that was where I lived.

They promptly called Pop Wood, the director, to come and get me.

John Wood was a big, sincere, and warm-hearted man. He and his wife ran the Home, and had for 20-plus years. We called him Pop, though at age eight I hadn't really had much to do with him. All I knew was that he was the boss, and that I was in trouble. Big trouble.

Pop came and picked me up in his 1952 Ford. He put me in the front seat with him. He drove me back to the Home. The whole trip back, he didn't say a word. In my mind, my punishment got worse with every passing block.

Finally, we got there. Pop turned to me. "Pat," he said, "do you know what you did?"

I burst into tears. My voice must have sounded like it was coming from a mouse. "Yes, Mr. Wood."

"Well," he said, "what do you think I should do with you?"

The mouse voice again. "Beat me, Mr. Wood."

Thinking back on this scene today, I suspect the hint of a

smile must have crossed Pop's lips. At the time I sure wasn't seeing any smile. I couldn't see anything through the tears. But his
response was the exact opposite of what I expected.

"Don't be silly, Pat. I'm not going to beat you. You're too smart
a kid to do something like this. I trust you not to do it again."

You can bet that I never did. You can also bet that, from then
on, Pop Wood had my undying respect and gratitude. Whatever
the man might ask to me to do, I would do. And whatever lessons he might try to instill in me, I would listen.

Unfortunately, Pop Wood left the Home when I was about
ten. And it was a couple of years later that I had my second mem-
orable experience.

The next director of the Home I didn't know real well; he was
pretty distant from most of the boys. I was 13, and in the throes
of early adolescence. One of the older kids gave me a playing
card. On it was a picture of a nude couple doing something. I
didn't know much about what they were doing, but I sure found
it interesting. There was a girl in my class at school that I was
starting to find interesting, too. I got the idea that if I showed her
that playing card—well, who knew what might happen? So I did.

Big mistake. *Big* mistake. She told her parents about the dirty
playing card this boy from the Home had shown her. You can
imagine their reaction. They probably took about five seconds to
get to the phone and call the director (whom we always called
"Mr.," not "Pop" or any other nickname). Suddenly he wanted to
talk to me. Right now.

That day, though, there wasn't much talking. Only hitting. He
used a wooden paddle. And when he was through with me, I knew
I had been beaten. Everyone else knew it too, since I couldn't sit
down for a couple of days. I was not only hurt, I was utterly humili-
ated. For a while it didn't dispose me any too kindly toward the adult
world. Luckily for me and the rest of the boys, that director didn't
last long. The man who replaced him, Bill Hazelgrove, had all the
virtues of Pop Wood and then some. It was Bill, for the most part,
who kept me on the straight and narrow during my teenage years.

I had one other experience I think was important in helping me understand how to treat—or not treat—people. It happened when I was 14.

I was walking along on the grounds of the Home when a cab pulled up. The cabbie rolled down his window and asked for directions to Mrs. Kidd's cottage. I told him she was in Cottage 5, around the corner, and he started to pull away. Then he suddenly stopped, backed up, and rolled down his window again.

"By the way," he said, "is there a kid here by the name of Pat Kelly?"

"Yeah," I said. "That's me. I'm Pat Kelly."

"Well," replied the cabbie, "I'm your father." And then he rolled his window up and drove off.

It turned out my dad was nervous about meeting me, figuring I wouldn't want to see him. But I was excited: Here was the father I'd never known. I went in to the office of the Home and inquired about him. They gave me his phone number. I called him up. I told him I wanted to see him, that I wanted to know who he was. He was pleased, and made arrangements for me to come over and visit for a weekend. He picked me up in his cab and we went out to his house.

We had a great time. I met his second wife and their son, who was close to my age. My father turned out to be a fine craftsman and hobbyist. He showed me ships he had built and put into bottles. He had an unbelievably elaborate model train set. The layout must have been 40 feet square, with some 18 different trains. Wow! I was so impressed I could hardly stand it. When he drove me back to the Home, he promised we'd get together again soon.

We didn't. He never called. I didn't see him again until years later, when he was dying.

So you can see why some things are important to me, and why my colleagues and I have always tried to build them into PSS. One is that idea about how it's easier to ask forgiveness than permission. We never punish people for making an honest mistake, or for screwing up. Another is the idea that I mentioned earlier in the book, the *soft landing*. If a person is promoted into a new job, and if that job doesn't work out, he or she always has another job waiting. A third value: We do what we say we're going to do at PSS. It's the only way to build a relationship of trust among people.

But it's a funny thing about values in a company. You can't just preach them. You can't just post them up on the wall. You certainly can't put them into a manual of rules and regulations and expect that everyone will suddenly say, oh, yeah, *that's* the way we ought to behave. Values have to be lived and breathed. They have to be taught and retaught.

Mostly, I've left the discussion of PSS's specific techniques to the next section. It's in those later chapters that you'll read about our Challenge Game, our Blue Ribbon tour, our interviewer's guide for foolproof hiring, and all the other tools that can help you build a faster company. But there's one I want to lay out right here, in the building-blocks section, because it's so important. In a way, it's the foundation on which the other techniques rest.

We call it the *Top 20*. It's a statement of our values.

PSS's Top 20 goes back to 1985, just a couple of years after we started the business. That year, all the leaders got together for a retreat on Amelia Island, near Jacksonville. We sat around on a porch there. And we talked for four hours straight. What would this company of ours stand for? People would throw out ideas. We'd bat them around. Eventually we came up with a list that we all agreed on. Some of the values had to do with our objectives as a business—getting enough of that food and water so that we could survive and grow. Most of them focused on how we wanted to treat our customers and each other—how we wanted to work together and what we wanted to provide the people who bought from us.

Here is the way the list reads today. It has changed little since 1985.

PSS'S TOP 20

To: **SERVICE** all our customers like they are the only one we have.

RECOGNIZE our people as our most valuable asset.

ALWAYS communicate without fear of retribution.

ENCOURAGE ideas and creativity at all levels.

ENCOURAGE self development and individual entrepreneurship.

ALWAYS strive to share the wealth.

ALWAYS promote from within first.

EARN profits and value for our entrusted shareholders.

PROVIDE an environment of trust and honesty.

MINIMIZE excuses and maximize getting the job done.

INVOLVE family in all social aspects of the company.

ENCOURAGE and develop pride and esprit de corps.

ENCOURAGE all PSS people to be shareholders.

TREAT all company assets like they are your own.

SUGGEST and encourage better ways of doing things.

MINIMIZE paperwork and memos.

BE professional at all times.

ANTICIPATE and capitalize on market needs.

DO what's best for all PSS.

RECOGNIZE PSS as a family that cares.

By itself, of course, this is just a list. What matters is what you do with your list, how you incorporate it into the day-to-day operations of the company. But this isn't as hard as it seems. In fact, there are only three requirements.

Requirement 1: Communicate the Values

At PSS, every single employee has a card in his or her wallet with the Top 20. You'll find it posted on the wall at every branch. When I'm talking to our people in the field, I'll often ask them to name a couple of the Top 20. Believe me, it's a part of our culture that would be hard to miss. We make sure new employees see it and understand it. We make sure veteran employees are constantly reminded of it.

Requirement 2: Implement the Values

By themselves, values are just statements of the way you'd like things to be. It's when you start to implement them that people begin to take them seriously.

Take that item about promoting from within, for example. At PSS, almost every one of our leaders is a PSS person, someone who has come up through the ranks. In fact, there were only four occasions on which we hired someone at the senior level from outside. Those were times when we needed a level of skill and experience that we just didn't have.

Still, we've profited enormously from the talent we've uncovered and developed in our own organization. I think of a guy like Gene Dell.

Gene joined us soon after PSS was launched. He was in his early twenties, and he hadn't been to college. At the time, he was selling lumber. We hired him as a trainee and put him to work driving a truck.

Over the years, Gene drove that truck and did a stint in the warehouse. He worked as a sales rep. When he moved into a leadership role, he went wherever he was needed, whether it was opening up new branches or taking over old ones. In just a few years, he had worked his way up to regional vice president of

PSS, running our largest region. Today, he is president and CEO in charge of the Diagnostic Imaging division. A few years from now, that will be a billion-dollar business.

Gene may be the most dramatic example of internal promotion at PSS, but there are plenty more. In fact, we make a point of offering advancement to every employee who wants a chance and who can show us that he or she has what it takes. If you start with us as a truck driver, for example, and you want to move into a sales or customer-service role, we'll move heaven and earth to give you the opportunity. If you succeed in one of those slots, you'll be considered for leadership training. *No one* is required to have a college degree or an MBA to advance at PSS. All you have to do is show us you deserve a chance. We'll be sure to give you one.

It's the same with the other values: We take them as a guide for action, and we try to implement them in every possible way. Involve family? Spouses are always invited to our employee picnics—usually held at a theme park—and national meetings. An environment of trust and honesty? That's one reason we practice open-book management; when people see all the numbers, they know we're not trying to keep any secrets. Share the wealth? You'll read in Chapter 15 exactly how we do it.

Requirement 3. Make No Exceptions!

Values are inconvenient. You have to honor them all the time, not just when it's easy to do so. Sometimes they force you to make hard, gut-wrenching decisions. But you can't make exceptions. If we fired just one person for going over the boss's head, for example, then that statement "*Always* communicate without fear of retribution" would be worth exactly nothing. And if we tolerated just one leader who didn't treat people in accordance with the Top 20, pretty soon we'd have cynicism so thick you could cut it with a knife.

I learned early on just how hard it can be to stick to a set of values. It happened when one of my early partners started acting like an autocrat.

My partner was a friend. He had put his money and time into PSS. He was a great sales rep, and pretty soon we moved him into a leadership role. But his style was exactly the opposite of what we wanted to see in the company. It was, *I'm the boss, so you'll do what I tell you to do.* There are any number of values on our list that this style is inconsistent with. At a minimum, he wasn't treating his people as if they were the company's most valuable asset.

Anyway, my partner was running one of our biggest branches. His primary responsibility was sales; the guy in charge of operations was named Chuck. We all thought Chuck was doing a great job. But one day Chuck came into my office and exclaimed, "Pat, I just got fired!"

I was dumbfounded. "Fired? Why?"

It took Chuck a minute, but he finally blurted out, "I guess because the coffee pot got left on last night."

Say what? I couldn't believe my ears. But Chuck said it again: It was the coffee pot.

"Wait a minute," I said. "Have a seat." Then I went over to the branch and asked my partner what was going on. No doubt my voice betrayed my incredulity. "You're firing Chuck because the coffee pot got left on?"

He got his back up. "That's right."

It was the start of a rapid-fire dialogue. "So what?" I asked.

"This building could have burned down!"

"Did Chuck leave it on or did an employee leave it on?"

"It doesn't matter. He's the manager here. He's responsible for that."

"If that's the case, you're the general leader—I should fire you for that coffee pot."

"Well, he's directly responsible for what happened."

I was getting more and more incredulous. "You can't fire somebody because the coffee pot was left on! We've got insurance in case the building burns down. You can't fire somebody for that."

"Well," said my partner, "he's also got other problems."

"Like what?"

"He bought a fifty-dollar file cabinet without asking me."

I shook my head. "You can't fire somebody for buying a fifty-dollar file cabinet, either. You can't do that."

Now it was my partner's turn to get exasperated. "Well," he said, "it's either him or me. Take your choice."

At that point my partner owned a lot of PSS stock. He was not only a friend, he had been an ally. I gave in. I said, "Okay, fine, you can fire him. Who are you going to promote?" Of course, he didn't have a replacement.

I went back to my office. There was Chuck, waiting word on what happened. Gloomily, I said, "Chuck, you really did get fired."

He was pretty gloomy too. "What am I going to do?"

"I don't know," I replied. "I guess you'll have to be my secretary!"

I actually did hire Chuck as a secretary, just until we could find something else for him to do. Pretty soon he was able to go to a different branch, and eventually to other branches around the state. He had a great career with PSS, and just recently retired.

What I learned from that, though, was that you can't make exceptions to your values, even when it's hard to stick to your guns. Because it was only a little while later that my partner got into another dispute involving an employee. Once again he was acting in haste. Once again he announced that it was either him or the employee.

This time it was him. We were sorry to lose him, but it was more important to keep to the company's values. Because the fact is that if you *do* communicate the values, implement them, and stick to them through thick and thin, you'll be doing something that's very unusual in the business world.

You'll be creating an organization that means something, that stands for something, that people care about and want to be a part of. You'll be building a business that attracts and keeps the best people.

You'll also be creating a company in which people can actually relax and enjoy their work. They can have a good time because they know they're a part of it and that they'll always be fairly treated. Later in this book you'll find a chapter on having fun. We want everyone to have fun at PSS, and I think we've come up with a lot of creative ways to encourage people to have fun. But the values come first. No one is going to have fun in an organization that treats its people poorly.

I think that's what I learned at the Boys Home. If you treat people right, if you include them and welcome them and teach them and help them reach their potential, your organization will succeed. And it will help make the world a better place.

So there you have it: the four building blocks of a faster company.

The building blocks are simple enough in concept. But they're hard to implement. At least they must be, because there are so few faster companies around. Maybe it's because you have to throw out most of the old ways of doing things and invent your own.

Alternatively, of course, you can learn from our experience, just as we've learned from the experience of other great companies. You can swipe our tools and techniques. In fact, everything you'll read about in the next section is a down-and-dirty, time-tested, hands-on method that you can use for building a faster company. And you're welcome to them.

Many thank-yous are due. One goes to Dana Corp., which has its own version of the Top 20. (See what I mean about stealing ideas?) Many more go to people I worked for early in my career, who treated their employees the same way as my former partner. From them I learned how not to run a company.

The real thanks, though, have to go to the two men who took the place of the father I scarcely knew, and who taught me what it means to treat people right. Thank you, Pop Wood and Bill Hazelgrove.

PART THREE

Getting It Done
Eleven Commandments for Building a Faster Company

COMMANDMENT I

Hire *Great* People

Have you ever stopped to consider how your company does its hiring?

Think about it. Here's one of the most important parts of any business. The hiring process brings you the people who will produce your goods, deliver your services, and do your selling, accounting, and everything else that needs doing. These are the people who will interact with your customers. Ultimately, they're the people who will determine whether your business succeeds or fails.

So how do you go about this process?

Chances are you put up a "help wanted" sign and wait to see who shows up. You put an ad in the paper, then pick candidates from all the resumes that come in.

Chances are, too, that you hire for particular jobs. You advertise for an accountant, a software engineer, a machine operator, or a sales rep, with no expectation that the people who fill those jobs will ever do anything else.

And if your company is like most, the one thing you're looking for in an applicant is experience. Basically, you want somebody who has done exactly the same job for the past five years.

This is how businesses have hired people for most of the twentieth century. And it probably used to make sense. In old-style factories and offices, what you needed were warm bodies who showed up for work on time and did what they were told. If those warm bodies had already done the same job for several years, they were probably reliable. They could start producing right away, which was really all you wanted them to do.

But today's marketplace is different. Today, what you need isn't warm bodies, it's whole human beings.

If you want to build a company of CEOs, you have to hire people who are capable of becoming CEOs. People who want to learn, grow, expand their horizons, and take on new challenges, whatever their job descriptions may be. People who aren't afraid of hard work and responsibility.

And if you want to do things that your competitors just can't do, you don't want people who are used to operating the way everybody else operates. You want people who can learn the systems and procedures that give your company a real competitive edge. You want people who will take the extra step, who will go the extra mile, who will *care* whether the company succeeds or fails.

You don't wait for these people to come to you. You go out and find them.

I've said it before in this book, and I'll repeat it here: *People are a faster company's only real asset.* You want—you need—the very best people you can find. You don't really care about experience, because you'll teach them to do things your way. But you do care—a lot!—about the attitudes and values they bring with them. You can teach people *how* to accomplish great things. It's much harder to teach them to *want* to accomplish great things.

This chapter tells you how we find great people at PSS. Mostly

I'll discuss how we find and hire salespeople—we're a sales-driven company, so we naturally place much of our hiring attention on the sales side. But we follow the same general approach in hiring everybody, from warehouse employees to accountants. After all, who knows what job they'll be doing at PSS five years from now?

Where to Look

First I have to tell you where we don't look. We don't run ads in the newspaper. We're not content just to wait to see who shows up.

Sometimes we hire people from our competitors. It's not because they have experience in the industry; in fact, their experience has more than likely taught them a different way from the way we do things. How are you going to teach sales reps to make 30 calls a day, which is what we expect at PSS, when they have been making only 20 for the past 10 years? How are you going to teach them about no-hassle service when their previous employers required forms filled out in triplicate before they'd take anything back?

But given enough time, it can be done. When we acquire a company, we always offer its salespeople a job with PSS. We want them to stay, because they probably have a well-developed list of regular customers. And in fact we have had great success with our acquisitions and their experienced reps, once the reps embrace our culture and selling methods; over 30 percent of our sales force has come from acquisitions, and they are essential to our success.

But we know from experience that it takes a year or two to convince experienced salespeople what PSS customers value. Not everybody can do it. Not everybody is happy doing it. When veteran salespeople decide to leave because they really don't like the pace, we could easily be back at square one.

Which is why we like to hire *inexperience*. People who don't know what they can't do. People who *want* to work in a faster company, and who can learn the PSS way right from the start.

We find a lot of these people on college campuses, where we recruit heavily. We'll set up booths on Career Day right next to IBM or Procter & Gamble, and we'll talk to the young people about a career at PSS. Of course, candidates don't have to be young. One woman we recently hired was 44 years old. When her daughter graduated from high school and went off to college, this lady decided she'd go to college too. Talk about someone with drive!

And it isn't just on the campuses that we find people. Maybe a salesperson working in another industry gets wind of PSS and gives us a call. Maybe one of our leaders spots a man or woman who seems to have the right attitude and ambition and encourages that person to look into PSS. Friends and relatives of our current employees, when they hear about PSS, are likely to be interested in applying.

As the saying goes, if you build it they will come. If you create a company that offers people real opportunity and challenge, they'll hear about you and come looking for jobs.

The Foolproof Interviewer's Guide

The next step in hiring is figuring out who is right for your company.

For a while, we weren't very good at this. We were in the early throes of fast growth, and our branch leaders had a lot to do. So they'd hire people quickly and rely on our training program—see the next chapter—to wash them out if they weren't suitable. For a while we were losing 30 percent of our trainees. It wasn't what you'd call a cost-effective hiring process.

That was when we began utilizing what *Inc.* magazine writer Teri Lammers dubbed "the foolproof interviewer's guide." It's a behavioral interview guide developed for us by a consultant named Ed Ryan, who runs a company called Marketing Personnel Research Inc., in Chicago. I'm not sure the guide is totally foolproof, but it sure has helped us identify at an early stage the people who will contribute most to our company and fit in most easily with its culture. Here's how it works.

FORMAT

The guide is just a series of 30 or so questions. Beside each question are suggestions about what we want the interviewer to listen for and space to write in what he or she hears. This listening is important. Interviewees always try to answer questions the way they think you want them to. We're listening for answers that someone trying to psych out the process wouldn't usually predict. We also want to hear specifics: anecdotes, examples, and details. That lets the interviewer know if there's anything worth pursuing. Next to the *listen for* column is a *rating* column. We just ask the interviewer to put a plus or a minus in the box. Once the interview is complete, we can add up the pluses and minuses and get a pretty good sense of the candidate's prospects.

QUESTIONS

The guide starts out with a few questions to break the ice. We ask about one particular year in high school (eleventh grade) and about the candidate's family. We ask about a proudest achievement and whether he or she ever had to go out on a limb to do what was right. We're looking here for broad-based characteristics: values, attitudes, and the ability to communicate.

Then we move on to a series of questions designed to reveal particular behavioral traits and characteristics. We ask, for example, what kind of relationship the candidate would like to have with coworkers. We're hoping he or she will be a person who wants warm, open, friendly relationships—the kind we encourage at PSS—not just businesslike relationships. We ask what the candidate likes about being in sales. We're looking for answers such as "Independence" and "Unlimited earning potential." A lot of our candidates give the answer, "Talking to people." But at PSS we're wary of big talkers. We like people who are good listeners.

As the interview progresses, our questions focus on work habits, ideas about selling, and expectations, as well as on the interviewee's personal traits. What number of hours per week do candidates think it takes to make a good salesperson? Why do they want to come to work for this company? How would they persuade reluctant prospects to buy? This last, of course, is a classic sales-interview question. Even so, the candidate's response tells us a lot. The answer we want is something like, "By asking questions and finding a need." If candidates get that right, we know they're way ahead in the game. But a lot of kids reply, "I'll cut the prospect a deal." That's not what we want to hear.

WHAT WE LEARN

Part of what we find out is how candidates perceive selling, and how they evaluate their own skills. But we're also learning deeper information about candidates. In that "Have you ever gone out on a limb?" question, for instance, we're essentially asking whether their ethics have ever been put to a test. If so, that's a definite plus. We're learning about what they've done. Have they played competitive sports? Have they assumed leadership roles on the campus or in the community? Did they have to work their way through school? "Yes" answers to any of these questions are definite pluses where PSS is concerned.

We also learn a lot about attitudes. We learn, for example, whether our candidates are people who want to win in every situation they approach. That's a must: Sales is a gladiator business, and salespeople have to win more battles than they lose or they just won't survive. Another must: being able to handle rejection.

Some questions are designed to show whether they have the resilience a successful salesperson needs. Finally, we measure a candidate's maturity. We ask, for instance, "What is the most important goal around which you organize your life?" We're learning whether people have given that any thought—and, if so, what they really hope to accomplish.

There's a side benefit of our interviewer's guide, which is that it keeps us all on the same page. Our company has grown fast. It has facilities all over the United States and in several locations overseas. Hiring is done mainly by branch managers, many of whom are barely 30 years old. That decentralization is a key to our rapid growth, and we wouldn't have it any other way. But it's important that everyone who joins PSS undergoes a similar interview and has similar expectations about the company. The interviewer's guide helps standardize the hiring process without a lot of cumbersome bureaucratic rules and procedures.

Do Call Us, We Won't Call You

It's tough to get hired at PSS! And not just because we have so many applicants for our slots.

The process might start at that hiring booth on the campus. Say a personable, goal-oriented young woman named Gail comes up to our recruiter there and begins talking. Remember, we're there next to the big guys, and for a long time nobody had heard of us. So if Gail seems like an ideal candidate, we first have to persuade her that PSS is worth considering. No, we can't offer her what she'd make at Johnson & Johnson or P&G. All we can offer is work at a unique company and opportunities for rapid advancement beyond anything she'd ever find at a Fortune 500 company.

But that's where the sales pitch for PSS stops. When we're through chatting, we'll give Gail a card with a local number on it. We'll say, "If you're interested in PSS, give us a call." If we don't hear from her, chances are she's not the kind of person we would have wanted anyway.

But maybe we do get a call, and maybe we're interested in Gail on the basis of our preliminary conversations. At that point we'll invite her in to the local branch. The branch manager will do the interview, using the interviewer's guide. Now we'll have a better evaluation—but even if it's positive, we won't call her back. Why not? Simple. We want the kind of candidate who will call *us* back and say, *"Hey, how about that job? Can I come back for another interview?"* That's part of what we're trying to find out: How badly do you want this job? If you want it badly enough, maybe you can get it. But you have to want it.

So let's say Gail does call back and asks about a second interview. We liked her the first time around, so now the branch manager says, "Okay, you can have a second interview. Get in touch with the manager of the branch in the next city." Gail has to call that manager, set up an interview, and get herself over there. Now we'll have two pretty thorough evaluations—but the fact is, we're still only halfway through the process.

If Gail is a sharp candidate, she'll probably have figured out the next steps by now. First, she'll have to go out with one of our salespeople for a full day. That not only gives Gail a chance to see first-hand what's involved in the job and to talk with someone who has been doing it, it also gives our salesperson an opportunity to evaluate Gail's prospects with PSS. We take that evaluation as seriously as we take the evaluations of the leaders. Finally, Gail will have to interview with the regional vice president or some other corporate officer. Nobody is hired at PSS until he or she has been interviewed by an officer of the company.

A cumbersome process? You bet. Time-consuming? Yup: The whole process is likely to take six or eight weeks. It's pretty grueling on the candidates, too. We never call them back. We don't encourage them much.

But what this process gets us is something money just can't buy. It gets us *great people*. It gets us people who can take the initiative, make the calls themselves, and overcome the fear of rejection. It gets us people who have demonstrated drive, determination, and ambition—and who can impress a whole series of tough interviewers with their abilities. These are people who will be capable of selling at the level PSS expects. They're also people who will likely be able to take on larger responsibilities. As you'll see in later chapters, we grow our own leaders at PSS. The first step in that process is hiring people who have the capacity to be leaders.

Does it work? Well, the mythical Gail could be following in the footsteps of another ideal candidate, who isn't mythical at all: Charlie Alvarez. Charlie graduated from Florida State University in 1989. He joined PSS right out of college at age 22. He did his training in Dallas, got his first sales territory in Fort Worth, and then became sales leader of our branch in Nashville, Tennessee. In the next few years he took over a branch in south Florida, opened a new one in Miami, and was named vice president in charge of what was then our eastern region. As I write, he is running a $110-million business as vice president in charge of PSS's northern region. He has just turned 30.

The First Commandment: Hire great people. If you want a company of CEOs, you have to create a process that identifies and selects potential CEOs.

COMMANDMENT II
Nonstop Teaching and Learning

So, you bring great people on board. Then what do you do with them?

This is another area where a lot of companies flounder. They'll hire eager young recruits, assign them offices and supervisors, and then leave them to their own devices. If there's a training program (and there rarely is), it lasts maybe a week. The thinking seems to be, *They'll pick up what they need to know. Better for them to get the experience than be sitting in some classroom.*

I couldn't agree more about the value of experience. We provide a lot of it in our training program. But the real issue here isn't training techniques, it's a company's fundamental approach to the people who have just joined it.

The fact is, the conventional approach makes perfect sense—for ordinary companies. Individuals have been hired for specific jobs, with no expectation that they'll ever do much else. They usually come with several years' experience under their belts. So what kind of training do they really need? A little orientation to the way their new company does things, perhaps. A few days working under the watchful eye of a supervisor until they get up to speed.

At a faster company such as PSS, however, the whole concept is different. We're hiring CEOs. We're expecting that people will commit themselves to the company, help build it, and take on more and more responsibility as they learn and grow. Our whole competitive edge, moreover, is built on doing things differently from—and better than—our competitors. We'd be crazy to take raw recruits (or anybody else!) and throw them into the fray without any preparation. It'd be like sending a football team into a game before they'd learned the plays.

So we take training very, very seriously at PSS—and not just for recruits but for everybody. As in the previous chapter, I'll focus on salespeople. But these lessons apply to any group of employees who are critical to the success of your company. If you don't teach them to know more and be able to do more than your competitors' people, how can you expect your company to outstrip those competitors?

Basic Training

At PSS, our sales training program lasts 16 weeks. It's nearly four months of work and learning so intensive that you can only call it basic training.

Think about what basic training involves in the military. In a short time, young soldiers learn dozens of new skills, everything from how to address an officer to how to fire an automatic weapon. They work harder, mentally and physically, than they have ever worked in their lives. They learn intangibles such as loyalty and unquestioning obedience to orders. They come out of basic training—if they make it through—as different people. They're more knowledgeable, more experienced, more committed, and more mature. They're ready to assume the responsibilities of serving in the armed forces.

PSS isn't a military organization, and our version of basic training isn't military in nature. We want our people to think for themselves, for instance, rather than blindly follow orders. Still, our approach has a lot in common with the military's. We throw you in. We expect you to work harder and learn more than you ever have before. If you don't make it through, we're sorry—but we're not going to ease up. The only kind of people we want representing PSS are the kind of people who *can* make it through.

What's involved? Listen to a few of the people who have gone through it.

SCUT WORK

"I couldn't believe it!" Marty Ellis exclaims. "They put me to work cleaning bathrooms."

We knew that Marty was the kind of person we were looking for the day he showed up for his interview. He was working in Columbus, Ohio, in another industry at the time, and he was scheduled for an interview at our Philadelphia branch. That day, Philadelphia had one of the worst snowstorms in its history. But Marty had heard that a snowstorm was on the way, and he allowed plenty of extra time for his drive from Columbus. He showed up for his interview—on time—on a day when not many vehicles other than snowplows were out on the streets of Philadelphia.

So Marty's first assignment, like the first assignment of a lot of trainees, was to clean the bathrooms. Next, he might be asked to sweep up the warehouse, empty the trash cans, or wash the windows in the office. You wouldn't say that trainees exactly love this kind of duty. After all, these are young (and not so young) hotshots, with a track record of accomplishment. But they learn a couple of key lessons. This is all work that has to get done. If it is done by people at the branch, the branch won't have to hire a cleaning crew. That means their costs will be that much less, their profits that much higher, and their bonuses that much bigger. At PSS, we all work together. We do what needs to be done, and we all profit from it.

REAL WORK

Then we put our fledgling salespeople to work doing regular jobs. They drive trucks and deliver goods to customers. They work in the warehouse, stocking shelves and picking orders. What do they learn?

- *Products.*   "You'd go into the warehouse and look at needles," remembers Becky Witt, who is now our marketing manager but was once a sales trainee. "You'd see they came fifteen gauge through thirty gauge. So then you'd have to figure out what *gauge* means." PSS carries thousands of products, and nobody can remember all of them. But salespeople who have picked items off shelves and delivered them to doctors' offices know them better than salespeople who have just looked at catalogs. They also learn which products are most important, even a mundane item like the paper that goes on a doctor's examining table. "When you're pulling items off shelves," says Becky, "you see, wow, we sell a *lot* of table paper. So later, when you're selling, you'll say, 'Do you need any table paper?' It's invaluable."

- *Customers.*   Driving a truck gets the young salespeople into the doctors' offices. They learn what goes on there. They see what's important to customers, and how they operate. They come to understand why, for example, doctors might want no sales calls or deliveries between 11:00 A.M. and 1:00 P.M., which are often their busiest hours. They can also begin learning from physicians. A trainee might ask the doctor what a particular piece of equipment is for, or exactly how the doctor uses the microscope. Most physicians enjoy doing a little teaching if they have the time, and it's another chance for the novice reps to learn their trade.

- *What their coworkers' jobs are like.* No doubt you've seen it in other companies: the classic split between sales and operations. According to sales, operations is always screwing up, mixing up orders and delivering late. According to ops, salespeople promise their customers the moon and have no clue what's involved in making good on their promises. At PSS, we try to bridge that gap right away by putting sales trainees in their future colleagues' jobs. They learn first-hand how hard the jobs in operations can be.

- *Resilience.* "It's always been the philosophy here that you start out doing everything, and when you get out there selling there's nothing that can make you feel bad." The speaker here is Susan Parker, who helps run the PSS University (see the next page) and is another veteran of the sales-training program. "You've emptied trash cans. You've driven trucks and stocked shelves. You can handle *anything*. When the door gets slammed in your face, you just walk away smiling."

PRODUCT KNOWLEDGE AND SELLING SKILLS

During the days, trainees are driving their trucks or working in the warehouse. Nights, they're expected to study and *learn*. Trainees get worksheets with key PSS products. They'll be expected to call manufacturers' 800 numbers and ask questions. Once a week, we'll test them on their product knowledge, and we'll expect high scores. Nobody gets through a sales training course at PSS without knowing one helluva lot about what we sell.

We also begin teaching selling skills during basic training.

"Once a week we'd work on our sales skills, trying to sell a product," says Becky Witt. "You'd grab the warehouse manager and say, 'I want to sell you Ninja Turtle Band-Aids.' " Today, every branch's sales leader is charged with teaching trainees the basics of selling, through regular instruction and role playing.

Once the trainees have been in a branch for several weeks, we'll make an evaluation. Do they work hard and hustle? Are they putting in the time needed to learn everything that's expected of them? Are they consistently scoring well on the product tests? If so, they're ready for the next step.

PSS University

You've heard of McDonald's Hamburger University. And you've probably seen or read about a lot of other corporate training centers. Most big companies have them these days. We stole the idea, even though at the time we were a relatively small organization. We think you're never too small to take training seriously. And if you do, there's no substitute for a *place* where people come to do nothing but learn. A place dedicated to teaching and learning gives you three advantages. One, you can impart a lot of information in a short period of time. Two, it's a unique opportunity to convey your company's culture. People learn what's important about your business, and they learn it in all the same way and at the same time. Three, people learn from each other and make friends, just as on a college campus. The experience creates bonds that extend throughout the organization—and that can last throughout a person's career with PSS.

Sales trainees typically spend a week at PSSU after eight or ten weeks at a field company. They've seen and done enough to know what's involved in selling for the company. But are they ready to make the commitment? At PSSU, we'll test them, challenge them, and even try to wash them out. We'll immerse them in sales training and in PSS's culture. We'll teach them the details of PSS's systems. If they make it through the university, they're on their way to becoming full-fledged sales reps. And we'll know they're as qualified for the job as we can possibly make them.

Specifics? Here's what the sales trainee experiences at the university:

PERSONALITY TESTING

At this point, it helps both the rep and the company if we learn more about their individual strengths and weaknesses. Do they have the right skills for a sales rep, or are they better suited to some other job? More important, do they have the will to sell? Can they take the rejection that's involved? We never use the personality tests alone to wash people out, but they sometimes help us identify trainees who are having doubts. You'd be surprised at the number of people who make it this far but then decide they really aren't that interested in selling or really don't want to work as hard as PSS expects them to. Ultimately, despite all our screening, about 20 percent of the people who enter our training program will make the decision to leave.

Personality tests have another benefit: Successful salespeople understand their own personalities and the personalities of the customers and prospects that they're working with. Our testing system classifies people as talkers, doers, pacers, and controllers. Salespeople typically fall into the *talker* category. But when they're explaining a new piece of equipment to a doctor—most of whom we'd classify as *doers* or *controllers*—they're not going to get anywhere by drowning them in words. They have to have facts and figures at their command. They have to get right to the point, explain exactly what the equipment does and why it's worth the doctor's attention. Learning about the different personality types helps the trainees understand not only themselves but the kinds of people they'll be selling to.

PSS AND ITS MARKETPLACE

One of the university's instructors teaches about PSS's culture: where the company came from, why it works the way it does, and what its values and beliefs are. We don't have a policy manual, so this is a great way to communicate how PSSers do things and how they treat one another. Another instructor gives lessons on PSS's marketplace. He or she will explain managed care and other industry trends, explain the Clinical Laboratories Improvement Act (CLIA) and OSHA regulations. All told, the testing and this introductory material take about a day.

SELLING SKILLS

Next we spend a couple of days teaching them a six-step selling program known as IMPACT. We didn't invent it (naturally!). It was developed by a man named Bill Brooks, and we bought it and adapted it. Essentially, it breaks the sales process down into six steps: Investigate, Meet, Probe, Apply, Convince, and Tie Up. This isn't a book on sales training, so I won't go into the details. But it's important for us all to learn the same process, for a simple reason: It lets us help each other. When a sales rep fails in a sales call, for instance, we can often analyze what happened, figure out at which step the rep lost the call, and help develop an action plan. This process fits well with PSS's culture because it teaches reps to listen, to identify customers' needs, and only then to explain how PSS can meet those needs.

Once we've explained the basics of the process, the trainees do a lot of role playing. They'll learn a section and then we'll role-play with a video camera capturing the interaction. It's amazing: When we play it back, the instructor almost doesn't have to do much teaching. The trainees themselves can see where they succeeded and where they failed. They come up with great ideas for improving their presentations. Sure, it's hard at first. But selling is hard. And everybody in the class is in the same boat. If they can survive two days of role playing and learn from what they see, they're one big step closer to becoming a successful rep.

NUTS AND BOLTS

On the last day, we teach them exactly how a PSS rep operates. We give them their laptop computers and teach them how to put in orders, retrieve the information the computers contain, and so on. We teach them how to organize a territory: the number of doctors they have to be seeing, how many to see each day, how to work a building efficiently, and how to organize their files. We give them the financial tools they'll need to do full cost-benefit analyses for customers interested in buying equipment. When the rep is through, he or she can talk intelligently about such topics as depreciation and the lease-versus-buy decision, as well as about the equipment's medical function and performance.

The University is an intensive experience. When the trainees leave, they have all the tools they need to become sales reps. But they're still green, so we send them to a new branch where they'll be paired with a veteran sales rep. For the next several weeks they'll make sales calls. It won't be long before they're ready for territories of their own.

At PSS, learning and teaching never stop.

Leaders, for example, go to PSS University for a *leadership development* program (more on this in the next chapter). Veteran salespeople go there for sessions we call *Experts Only*, where we emphasize the skills required to sell complex medical equipment, and for a program known as *Profit College*, which teaches a variety of techniques for increasing gross margins. Operations people come in for special training, too. All told, there must be about eight formal educational programs running at PSS all the time. The University costs us about $3 million a year, or about 5 percent of our corporate budget. It's worth every dime.

Of course, not all the learning takes place at the University. At every sales meeting, we'll have manufacturers in to give seminars on the latest equipment. And everybody in a branch is exposed to a constant stream of information about the company's financials (see Chapter 12). But what's really important isn't the specifics, it's that we build in what I call the *habit of learning*. From the initial training program on, we expect that people will continue learning and eventually teach others what they know. This process of continuing education is what transforms people who are promising but inexperienced into the kind of people who can staff a faster company, such as PSS.

The Second Commandment: Commit to nonstop teaching and learning. Education is what enables people to reach their full potential—and a faster company needs people who can be peak performers all the time.

CHAPTER

9

COMMANDMENT III
Grow Your Own Leaders

Have you ever noticed the number of young, fast-growth companies that burn out like shooting stars? They start up with a hot new idea and get plenty of customers. They expand rapidly, adding new customers and product lines and facilities. They attract attention in the industry and maybe make some magazine's list of up-and-coming young companies.

Then, *pfffft*. They're gone.

The problem with these companies isn't finding customers. They've already demonstrated their ability to do that. And the problem is rarely money. There's always capital available to finance the growth of a successful business.

Almost invariably, the problem is people. The entrepreneur who started the business doesn't have the skills to run a bigger company. He or she can't attract (or can't keep) seasoned leaders. Before long, branches and departments and business units are being run by people who don't have the necessary skills, training, or temperament. Things turn chaotic. Key employees leave. The company begins to flounder.

The same scenario is often played out in older, larger businesses. Market conditions change. A company finds itself struggling. Suddenly, its leaders are uncertain about what to do. The most imaginative and talented ones leave in search of greener pastures, leaving their less-skilled colleagues behind. The same downward spiral begins.

The fact is, *nothing is more important for the long-term health of a business than its leadership*. And I don't mean just the two or three people at the very top, I mean the people who lead every branch and department throughout the organization. If a company is growing fast, it needs a constant supply of leaders to take on new tasks and territories. If a company is more mature, it needs leaders who can guide it through the twists and turns of today's marketplace.

Most companies, of course, use the word *managers* to describe the individuals I'm referring to as leaders. Frankly, I think that's part of the problem. People who are called managers think that their job is to manage the employees who report to them. It's the manager's job to hand out assignments. It's the manager's job to tell everybody else what to do. *In a faster company, nobody needs to be told what to do.* Employees need coaching, sure. They need help when they encounter a situation they've never confronted before. They need someone to show them the big picture and to make sure nobody's working at cross purposes with anybody else.

You manage things. You lead people. People need leadership and they don't need management. At PSS, the people responsible for our branches, regions, and departments are always called *leaders*, not managers. It's a reminder of what their real role is.

So where do you find leaders? The answer is that you don't. You grow them. They're in your organization right now. All you need to do is identify them and develop them.

Leadership School

I have to admit, it took us a while to learn this lesson. Especially the "develop them" part.

Like a lot of companies, we used to have a simple approach to leadership. We figured that if you were good at your job, you'd automatically be a good leader. So the best salespeople were thrown into sales-leadership slots. The best operations people were promoted to run operations. The best branch leaders were given responsibility for bigger branches or even for whole regions.

As with any group of people, there were a few who rose to the occasion. They learned fast, on the job. They succeeded. But many more found themselves in deep water before they had ever learned to swim. They splashed around helplessly. They quit and went back to what they were doing before. We had a *huge* turnover problem in our leadership ranks, and it was all because we didn't realize that leaders are made, not born.

That was when we started our leadership school.

It takes place at PSS University, just like the sales-training program. It even has some features in common.

For one thing, it starts with personality testing. Just as we test trainees for sales aptitude, we test would-be leaders for leadership skills. We think this is pretty important. The candidates who come to the school, after all, are a mixed bag. They have been successful in their jobs or they wouldn't be there—but that, as we had discovered, is no guarantee that they'll make a good leader. Maybe they're too ego-driven (many top salespeople are). Maybe they aren't good at solving other people's problems. Then, too, some of the candidates are there not because they've been outstandingly successful but because they have expressed a burning desire to take on a leadership role. We agree to give them a shot—but we want to make sure they have the ability to grasp what they'll need to succeed as a leader.

After the personality testing, we take them through the IMPACT sales-training program again. It's partly to refresh their memory, but it's mostly to help them learn how to communicate the IMPACT language and process to trainees. We want to make sure that they understand it well enough to teach it. (As any teacher will tell you, that means understanding it very well indeed.) Then we spend a day discussing leadership. We talk about the role of the leader as described by Plato, Dostoevsky, and Martin Luther King, Jr., as well as by contemporary authors such as Warren Bennis and Max DePree. We also do problem solving. In one session, they solve problems as individuals. We evaluate how they do. Then we teach them a process for problem solving as a team. That's what we want them to do when they're functioning as leaders in the field, and the whole point of the leadership school is to teach people new behaviors. Finally, we take them out to a challenge course and do some team building. It's a great bonding experience for the people who go through it.

At the end of the sessions, we'll sit down with all the candidates individually and review their scores with them: where they're strong, where they're weak, and what we think they'd be best suited for. At this point about 40 percent of the candidates decide not to go forward into leadership, while 60 percent do want to move forward. Sometimes in that 60 percent there's an individual that we don't think will make it. We'll counsel that person: Here's where your weaknesses are, here's why we don't think you'd be successful as a leader. We'll explain the high-risk nature of a leadership role at PSS, and ask them if they're sure that's what they really want to do. But if the candidate says, "I don't care what the test shows, I want a chance," then we'll nearly always give him or her a chance. And once they decide to go on, nearly everyone who has been through this program succeeds.

Creativity Week

Suppose you came in to work one day and discovered that the batteries in all your delivery trucks had been stolen. Your customers don't want to hear about your problems; all they want is the same-day service they've been promised. What do you do?

At PSS, every young leader is expected to read three key books and study and discuss some 50 real-life problems like this—and then teach the lessons to another group of young leaders. All this takes place not at the University but on a boat, cruising down the intracoastal waterway toward south Florida. We call it Creativity Week.

We sort of stumbled on the idea for Creativity Week. It was back in 1989, when we were first coming up with the goal of creating the first national physician-supply company (see Chapter 3). We needed to build consensus around the goal, so we'd ask people in leadership positions to go out on the boat and talk it over. At the same time, we'd discuss some of the operational issues and problems we were experiencing as we grew, and we'd try to come up with solutions for them. Over time, we wrote up case studies on particular problems like the preceding one— something that a leader would have to use some creativity in order to solve.

Today, Creativity Week is a key part of our leadership training. Leaders who make it through the University and decide to go on are assigned to a branch. But then—usually within the first six months—we ask them back to Florida for Creativity Week. They're asked to read *The Goal*, by Elihu M. Goldratt (North River Press, 1994), *A Whack on the Side of the Head*, by Roger Van Oech (Warner Books, 1992), and *The Seven Habits of Highly Effective People*, by Stephen Covey (Simon & Schuster, 1989). Then they get on the boat, three at a time.

On the first day, John Sasen, Gene Dell, or I teach the group. We lead them in a discussion of the books, and we go over the case studies. There's that one about the batteries, which elicits ideas ranging from "buy new batteries" to "use the employees' cars for delivery." Most of the case studies are a little more complex; they're down-and-dirty, nuts-and-bolts, real-world issues, exactly the kind of small but critical problems that every leader must solve day in and day out. For example:

Dr. Harold Brantley [all these names are fictitious] is one of PSS's best customers, but has a tendency to get behind on his bills. Tom Arnold is the leader of the branch and has to put Dr. Brantley on credit hold nearly every other month. John Dandy is the sales rep, and John is pulling his hair out trying to keep Dr. Brantley off credit hold.

Right now it's March, and Dr. Brantley is on credit hold. John asks Tom for relief because he is confident Dr. B. can work out of it. Then Dr. Brantley's office calls up: They need syringes urgently, because of a rash of inoculations. Customer service informs Tom. Tom says sorry, no way can they ship the product out. Dr. Brantley is furious. He has been slow, he knows, but he always pays his bills, including the service charges for late payment. He tells his nurses never to buy from PSS again.

If you were Tom, what would you have done?

Or:

Mark could not get Steve Block motivated. Sure, Steve was on commission and not hurting the company, but he was missing his forecast. Mark had his hands full. Corporate had just pulled a couple of his top sales pros as leaders and had given him a bunch of rookies. To add insult to injury, one of the rookies Corporate gave him a year ago was not making it, and Mark had positioned a trainee to replace this failing rep.

One afternoon at 2:00 P.M. Mark was returning from a customer and decided to stop by Steve's house. His wife had a gift for Steve's wife and had asked Mark to drop it off. What a surprise to find Steve in blue jeans, watching soap operas. Steve made excuses, but Mark blew him away and stormed back to his car.

With all the transition that's going on, does he fire Steve now? What would you do?

But it isn't just day-to-day problems that we ask them to solve; we also discuss issues of corporate growth and strategy. One case study reads like this:

At PSS, Al Jones has an opportunity to decide which market PSS will start up in next. His choices are:

Cleveland.   There are two local companies in the physician market. One does $6 million with 16 reps and does a great job. Three national chains are in the market and are aggressive pricers.

Boston.   A strong doctor house in Metro Medical: $10 million with 24 reps. Metro is a service machine but has no real price competition. Two national mixed houses are in the market, but neither is doing much. Metro is employee owned and has been around a long time. A few of their sales reps, however, are unhappy with their commission program.

Salt Lake City.   The crossroads of America, and every national house in town. Four major mixed houses, all aggressively fighting on price. No doctor house per se, but a three-man operation known as Crossroads Medical.

Al asks your advice on which market to choose. What do you tell him, and why?

The discussions provoked by these case studies are fascinating, illuminating, and instructive—especially because after the first day, it's the young leaders themselves who are doing the teaching. On day two, for example, we get another group of three on board. Now it's the people who were there on day one who are the teachers instead of John, Gene, or me. On day three, the day one people leave and the day two group will teach yet another group. And that's the way it proceeds, all the way down to Miami or Key West.

Some 40 or 50 people a year go through this experience. (As

we've grown larger, we've had to supplement the boat trips with sessions held in one place—usually the Florida Keys.) It teaches people how to be PSS leaders, stretches their thinking, and gives them a chance to spend time with John, Gene, and me and with each other. We wouldn't trade Creativity Week for anything.

PSS has grown phenomenally. We have added new centers year after year, recorded sales growth of 50 percent or more, and recently branched out into whole new areas. How could we possibly have done this without plenty of new leaders in the pipeline? We say to all our employees: *We don't care how young or inexperienced you are. If you show us you have what it takes, we will teach you to be a leader. And PSS will be a stronger, faster company because of what you contribute.*

The Third Commandment: Teach people in your company to be leaders. A faster company needs leaders (not managers!) throughout the organization—and the best ones are always home-grown.

CHAPTER 10

COMMANDMENT IV
Grow Your Organization

Okay, so the phrase "grow your organization" is a little cryptic, but I didn't know what else to call this commandment. I also didn't want to leave it out, because it's important and often overlooked. Businesspeople often forget that a company is just human beings in jobs, and how well the company performs depends on how well those human beings are matched up with the jobs the company needs done.

Here's what I'm driving at. You can have the best people in the world, carefully selected and well-trained. You can have a deep reservoir of leadership. But if you don't *deploy* these people well, you're not taking full advantage of what you have. You have to put individuals where they'll contribute the most to the organization's growth. That usually means putting them where they'll be challenged and have to stretch. You have to move them when they're ready for new responsibilities. You have to be sure that you always have enough people in reserve so that your organization never slows down. This is the only way a faster company can function at top speed all the time. You *must* have people who can go exactly where they're needed—and then you must make sure that the organization puts them there, quickly.

In this chapter I'll tell you exactly how we do it—because, believe me, we have learned a lot about deploying the troops.

Fast Assignments

Let's take a sales trainee, just out of college, and call him Dave. Maybe Dave graduated from the University of Florida, as many of our sales reps have. He goes through the hiring process and is assigned to our Orlando branch for training. If he then completes PSS University successfully, he'll be assigned somewhere else—Atlanta, say—for further training. That's where he'll be paired with a veteran sales rep and start making sales calls.

But Dave is really waiting for a territory. And when a territory opens up, we'll ask him to go there. Right away.

At PSS, "right away" *means* right away. As in *now*. We want you to have your bags packed, your car gassed up, your friends and family prepared for your departure. Don't believe me? Here's how Becky Witt remembers being assigned to her first territory:

> At the time, we were getting ready to move into the Texas area, out of Dallas. The operations trainee in the branch with me was saying, "You're going to Texas with me." I even called my parents: "I'm going to Dallas!" But you never know. In our trainee program you never know where you're going until they give you that call.
>
> Anyway, out of the blue, on a Tuesday night, I got a call. It was nine-thirty at night, and it was my leader. She said, "Becky, I have some news." I said, "Is this the call?" And she said, "This is the call. We need you in Savannah."
>
> Savannah! And I had thought I was going to Dallas. But then

the second shoe dropped. "And we need you there by eleven-thirty tomorrow morning." I was dumbfounded: "Excuse me?" But she repeated it. I had to be there by eleven-thirty the next day.

Well, I made it. I was in Savannah by eleven-thirty A.M. I had lunch with the rep who was leaving and rode with him the rest of the afternoon. That was Wednesday. Thursday and Friday I worked all day, then I drove back home and picked up the rest of my stuff. I went back to Savannah Sunday and went to work Monday.

We never want to assign reps too close to home. Working at PSS is demanding, particularly for a young person. You have to put in long hours. You have to focus on providing your customers top-notch service. In our reps' early years, we don't want them hanging out with their buddies too much, because it means they probably won't succeed at the job. For a while we tended to send people far away from home—too far—and it backfired. They'd get too lonely. Now we tend to assign them to a branch that's not too close to their homes but still within driving distance. It keeps things in balance, and it means that we aren't asking a kid from Mississippi to sell to doctors in Minnesota.

Incidentally, there's one secret to fast assignments: You have to keep people ready and waiting, in reserve—even if it takes a couple of months before they get a regular assignment.

For years I have belonged to a great organization called TEC (formerly The Executive Committee). It's a group of business owners and CEOs. We meet regularly to discuss our companies and our business problems. And for years I have been telling them how we keep a reserve army of about five percent of our salesforce. These are people who are all trained and ready to go, just waiting to be given a territory.

Some of my colleagues in TEC can't believe it and haven't been bashful about saying so. "What a waste of money," they'll say. "You've spent big bucks hiring and training these men and women. And you don't send them into the field right away? You're crazy!"

To us, though, this reserve of trainees is simply a cost of doing business, faster company-style. What are you going to do if a rep suddenly leaves? Put an ad in the paper and spend 16 weeks training somebody who answers the ad?

Hardly. We have people literally gassed up and ready to go. And when someone leaves, we'll have another person out there selling the very next day.

Fast Promotions

At PSS, you may not stay long in one place. In fact, we have a saying about that. (Sometimes I think we have a saying about damn near everything.) We say: *It's not the years, it's the mileage.*

Of course, not everybody moves. Plenty of PSS employees are long-time residents of their communities, with homes and families and everything else that ties people to a place. They stay at the branch they're associated with.

But the people who are on the way up in the company—particularly those who are just starting out—will find themselves on a fast track:

- If they succeed as a sales rep in their first assignment, we'll give them a bigger territory somewhere else if they want one. It'll happen after a year or two, not after five years.
- If they have qualified for a leadership role, chances are they'll have to move to a branch that needs a new leader. They'll go the minute an opportunity opens up.
- If they're leading a successful branch and they want to move up, we'll give them a chance to lead a larger or more challenging branch. And they won't have to wait five years for that opportunity, either.

The people who really climb aboard the fast freight train are those who really want to move up in the company and who show by their performance on the job that they have the ability to do it. We'll make sure these individuals gain a lot of experience in short order. We'll place them as leaders in a couple of different branches. We'll send them out into a brand-new territory to start up a new branch. We'll put them in charge of a region—a small one at first, then a larger one. Maybe they'll do a stint at our corporate offices in Jacksonville.

What makes this fast movement possible, of course, is our fast growth. We're always adding new branches and expanding the ones we have. But the flip side is true, as well: It's the fast movement of people that enables us to grow fast. You can't open a new branch if you don't have people to staff it. You can't grow a branch if you don't have people who can lead larger and larger business units. You couldn't possibly expand into a whole new part of the health-care business, as we have done, without leaders who have already gained a wide variety of experience within PSS.

Soft Landings

In the introductory chapter I mentioned what we call the *soft landing*. It's an indispensable element of our fast-moving deployment of our people.

After all, what are you doing when you give people the chance to move so far so fast? You're asking them to stretch. You're asking them to do things they haven't done before. You don't know if a good salesperson or operations specialist is going to be a good leader. You still don't know even if they pass the leadership course with flying colors. You can't know until they've done it for a while. It's the same with any move. Maybe a leader is comfortable with a $5 million branch and utterly out of his or her depth with a $20 million branch. Maybe an operations person should stay in operations and not try to move up to a corporate position. You really don't know until you put them there and see what they can do.

And you know what? If they can't do the job, you have to end the experiment equally fast.

See, we'll know quickly when somebody's not working out. We watch their numbers every month and keep a careful eye on people who aren't making their forecasts. We'll hear from the employees in a branch that the new leader doesn't have what it takes (see Chapter 14). Sometimes we'll hear directly from their customers. A sales rep or branch leader who has unhappy customers is a liability we can't afford. We'll make every effort to help that person: In fact, the regional vice president may be on the phone or in a branch nearly every day until the problem is corrected. But if it can't be corrected—if the person is clearly in the wrong job—then we'll move *very* quickly to find a replacement.

We can do this for one simple reason: *It's no crime to fail at PSS.*

If you don't work out in a new job after giving it your best shot, you can have your old job back. If there's another kind of opportunity that suits you better, we'll look for that. This is what we call our *soft landing*. It's the exact opposite of the up-or-out approach to careers practiced by the military and by many large corporations. We *want* people to stay with us. We want them to go as far in the organization as they possibly can. And we will *never* punish them for taking on a job that turns out to be beyond their abilities.

This practice allows us to keep some of our best people, people that we would otherwise lose. I mentioned Jim Boyd earlier. Jim joined us right after PSS was founded. He was a super sales rep. He led branches, engineered a couple of startups, and eventually became a regional vice president. Not all these steps worked out, and Jim sometimes had to move back to the job he came from. But he just kept learning from his experience and seeking out new opportunities. Today he is vice president of our diagnostic equipment division and one of the most valuable people anywhere in the company.

And Jim isn't unique. Take a guy named Don, whom we made a branch leader in Alabama. Don wasn't the most patient individual in the world, and before long it was clear to us that he had to be replaced. We assigned him to lead another branch, but within two years he had run into trouble there, also. Being in charge of a branch was obviously not Don's strong suit.

But all along, Don showed some extraordinary strengths. He is one of the smartest people I know. He can solve problems faster than any three ordinary people. Eventually we brought him to corporate and made him into a kind of teacher. Today, he visits branches. He identifies problems, helps the local people figure out solutions, and moves on to the next branch. He brings an incredible amount of value to the company in this capacity.

And where would we be if we didn't have soft landings? We probably would have lost Jim, and Don, and a hundred other people who could have contributed to PSS's fast growth. And we wouldn't be the faster company that we are today. It's people who enable you to grow fast and move fast. And it's deploying those people well that lets you stay at top speed all the time.

> *The Fourth Commandment: Grow your organization by deploying your people for maximum effectiveness. Move them fast, promote them fast, challenge them to do what they've never done before—and be sure they have a soft landing if they don't succeed.*

COMMANDMENT V
Open the Books (and Everything Else)

I wrote earlier (see Chapter 5) about how PSS is an open company. Open books. Open doors. No secrets. The reason is simple: Information is power. If you want people to think and act like CEOs, you have to make sure that everybody knows as much as possible about the company and how it operates. You can hire the best people in the world. You can train them within an inch of their lives. But if they don't have regular ongoing access to information, they won't be able to make smart decisions.

A lot of CEOs are beginning to understand this point, and most companies today are more open than they used to be. There's even a thriving community of open-book companies with its own conferences and regional get-togethers. But as even these companies are discovering, it isn't just a matter of putting information out there and expecting that suddenly every employee in the place is going to be well informed. Some employees don't have the educational background to understand much about the business. Others—many others—don't think it's their job. After all, when most people come to work every day, nobody's asking them to know or care much about the company that employs them. They're just supposed to perform a set of tasks, pick up their checks, and go home.

We have set out to change that situation at PSS. We tell people right from the start that part of their job is to know—to understand—what's going on in the company. Then we do everything we can to make it as easy (and as much fun) as possible.

Teaching Salespeople the Business

For us it starts (as does nearly everything else) with the sales reps.

At a lot of companies, a sales rep's job isn't much different from a clerk's. The reps take orders. The prices they can offer are pretty much fixed—if they want to cut the customer some slack to close a deal, they have to get an okay from the sales manager. And, of course, it has to be that way. The reps get paid their commissions on gross revenue, so if the sales manager wasn't looking over their shoulders they'd probably give away the store. Just like workers in an old-style factory, the reps aren't paid to think, they're paid to write down what the customer wants. If there are decisions to be made, they'll be made by the manager.

At PSS, we view our reps differently. We assume that they're entrepreneurs running their own little businesses. We want them to succeed in those businesses. Heck, we want them to succeed beyond their wildest dreams. So we make sure that they have all the information, training, and authority they need to do just that.

The first step is the training program described in Chapter 9. Sales reps learn about the products we carry and about selling skills—but they also learn how to run the business effectively. We teach them how to manage the gross margin, which is the number that will determine their commissions (and which most affects our profits). We give them classes in finance, so that they can help a physician do a return-on-investment analysis on a particular piece of equipment. We allow them total pricing discretion on individual items, so they can manage their accounts effectively.

Then we give them what we call their ICONs, for our Instant Customer Order Network—little laptop computers, activated with the touch of a pen.

From the customer's point of view, these computers are handy order devices. They make it possible for the sales rep to take an order quickly and then transmit it to the warehouse for same-day delivery. From the sales rep's point of view, the computers are much, much more. They're repositories of all the information the rep needs to run a successful business.

Using the ICON, for example, reps know exactly what each customer ordered and when. They know what the customer paid. They know customers' credit histories and whether they have anything on back order. If a rep wants to sell by gross margin, the computer will calculate prices. When an order is complete, the computer will tally up the rep's sales and margin for the day so far. It will compare actual sales to forecast sales, month-to-date and year-to-date. Every night, it will be updated with new pricing data, information on back orders, receivables, and so forth—everything a business owner needs to know.

The ICON demonstrates the power of information in the sales process itself. Say a customer is interested in a piece of equipment—an IMX chemistry analyzer, say, for performing prostate-cancer screens in the office. The computer can provide the customer with an online manufacturer's catalog, complete with full descriptions of features and benefits and analyses of competitive products. Then the rep can ask the doctor how many procedures he or she typically does each month, pull up the reimbursement codes for those procedures, and show exactly how much revenue the physician can realize by performing those tests with the new equipment. If the customer is still uncertain about the product, the rep can calculate exactly how long it will take to pay for itself.

We have a few reps at PSS who write as much as $3 million in business every year. We have many who write more than a million. They're bright, talented, hardworking salespeople, every one of them. Yet I'm absolutely convinced that one of the factors enabling them to succeed is that they have learned to be smart businesspeople. They can run their own businesses effectively because they have the information they need literally at their fingertips.

Information-Rich Operations

Companies in the distribution business are funny organizations. Like PSS, most are sales-driven. They depend on their salespeople. They lavish attention on their salespeople. Maybe I've given you the impression in this book that the only employees we have are salespeople.

If so, I want to correct it right now. We do love our salespeople. But like any distributor, we are only as good as the people who actually pick and deliver the goods, keep the accounts, and perform all the other tasks that make it possible for a sales rep to keep on selling. The operations side of our business is every bit as important as the sales side. If we slip up there, we will fail.

As I said, though, it's a funny combination. Salespeople are typically outgoing, gregarious, ego-driven, and ambitious. They always want the best for their customers and may not always stop to consider the details of what they're asking for. Operations people have to be steady, solid, and detail-oriented. They need to look at the whole picture, balance off one customer's needs against another's, and solve problems in ways that benefit the branch as a whole. When we're hiring in operations, we tend to value experience more than we value it in hiring sales reps.

I learned about the importance of good operations early on, even before PSS started up.

I was assigned by Intermedco to take over its Florida sub-sidiary, known as Surgical Supply. The operations leader at Surgical was a guy named Wayne. Wayne was the hardest-working person I'd ever seen in my life. He came in at seven o'clock in the morning. He stayed until seven at night. He didn't let up all day. The salespeople at Surgical loved him because he worked so hard.

When I arrived, though, one thing was crystal clear: This company was not well organized. The warehouse was a mess. Customers weren't being serviced well. First thing I did, I took off my coat and tie and went to work on the warehouse. For two weeks Wayne and I worked on the warehouse, and, finally, we got it organized. Then I tried to help Wayne see the importance of getting the trucks rolling on time. Deliveries had to go out every day. The trucks had to leave early enough to make a full round every day. In order to do that, you had to get them loaded up quickly.

We worked and worked at it, but the situation didn't improve. Finally, I made the decision that Wayne needed another job. I offered him a chance to go to Orlando—a smaller branch—and run operations there. Instead, he decided to leave.

At this point, the sales force was furious with me. Furious!

They called Rick, my boss in Houston, and told him I was making a big mistake. Rick called me and advised me to get Wayne back. I held the line. Rick said he might have to fire me if I didn't take Wayne back. I told him, go ahead. I was really sorry Wayne was leaving, and said so. But taking him back would be absolutely the wrong thing to do.

Finally, Rick agreed to back me. But then I had to get some-body to take Wayne's place.

I had met a guy named Lindsay, who at the time was living in Virginia. Lindsay didn't know anything about our business, but he had worked for a beverage bottling company, routing trucks.

He understood how to get product out the door. I talked to him and told him straight out, we'll teach you to understand our business, but you have to guarantee me that you can get product out the door. He said, "Pat, that I know." So I hired him.

Well, it was like night and day. Lindsay did exactly what he said. He got the trucks rolling. And what do you suppose happened?

Customers started buying more from us, because they knew they were assured of getting what they ordered.

The company grew from $3 million to $10 million in 3 years.

The salespeople who had wanted my scalp suddenly decided I wasn't such a bad guy after all.

They hadn't understood that Wayne, hard as he worked, didn't have the skills to run a smooth operation. Lindsay did. He got things organized and working. The systems he put in place made all the difference to that company.

Incidentally, I got a call from Wayne four years later, when I was in Houston. Oddly enough, it was Christmas Day. I had lost track of him, so I asked him where he was and how he was doing, and I'll never forget his response. "Pat," he said, "I'm in Waxahachie, Texas. I just graduated from ministry school, and I have my own church here. I just wanted to call to thank you for helping me find my right calling."

So one lesson I learned is that, as chief executive, you sometimes have to let people go, even when it's hard. You may even be doing them a favor. The other lesson is that there's no substitute in our business for an effective warehousing and delivery operation.

But there's a third lesson, and I really didn't learn this until later, when we at PSS began practicing open-book management. If you want a *really* effective and smooth operation, you have to get everybody involved. Truck drivers. Warehouse workers. The people in the office. They all have to understand what's important about the business. They have to see all the information that shows them how they're doing. Just as salespeople need all the information in their computers, the folks in operations need all the information that the branch leadership can make available. They have to see it, understand it, and care about it. Over time, we have developed some great tools and techniques for helping them do just that.

P&L MEETINGS

One thing we do is hold monthly meetings at each branch to review the P&L. These meetings are off-site, after hours, and voluntary. The branch leader will walk people through the income statement. They'll talk about any problems that may have come up: inventory problems, line items that are over budget, whatever. People will ask questions—any questions they want. Then they'll put their heads together and come up with solutions.

Just knowing the numbers has a significant effect on how people do things. Listen to Nick Pecoraro, leader of our New Orleans branch:

> We'll go through the line items. I might say, "Gee, we're a little high on electricity. Anybody know why?" People will chip in: "Maybe we didn't turn off the A/C when we left." Or, "Maybe we're leaving the lights on in that room that nobody's in now." It makes everybody think: if we're three hundred dollars high this month on electricity, and if you multiply that times twelve, that's thirty-six hundred dollars more that could fall to the bottom line.

That matters to everybody, of course: Everyone's eligible for a bonus, and nearly everyone's a shareholder. If profits aren't what they should be, everybody suffers.

Even so, I can imagine what you're thinking. *A meeting to go over the financials? After hours? Voluntary? Oh, sure. We'd be lucky to have three people show up!* And you're right, of course. Not many people love to think about numbers. Not many employees are used to taking responsibility for their employers' expenses. If open-book management is going to work, you have to make it fun.

THE CHALLENGE GAME

So, when we hold these meetings, we don't rent a conference room in some hotel. We go somewhere fun. An amusement park, maybe. A bowling alley, a miniature-golf arcade, a skating rink. We take everybody out for pizza or ribs. It's different every month, but we always have a good time. It's toward the end of the work day, and it lasts only an hour or so. So people can still get home to be with their families.

We do something else, too. We started it just a few years ago. We call it the *Challenge Game.*

See, when we began holding these P&L meetings they were boring. Even when people went off site, the meetings themselves were still a chore. People's eyes glazed over. Many employees didn't bother to come. We needed some way to make the meetings themselves fun. So we got together and created our own game. It's modeled on the TV show *Family Feud.*

You should see it in action! Picture a roomful of employees, divided into two teams, Red and Blue. A question comes up on the computer screen: "PSS provides same-day service within __ miles. The number-one answer is . . ." Maybe the team that has the question answers, "Forty miles." And the buzzer goes off: Wrong! If they answer, "One hundred miles by eleven A.M.," they'll get the beep—Right!—and they get four points. There are 100 points in each game, and each team builds up points. Over time, they can trade in points for watches, jackets, cameras, all sorts of prizes.

Corny? Maybe. But believe me, people really get into it. They'll be jumping up and down, yelling. They want to win. But they're also learning. How many branches does PSS have? Who is our chief competition? One month will focus on the financials. Another will focus on PSS's culture, or on its marketplace. They have to keep up with what's going on in the company, and they have to learn the numbers they see on the P&L. Before each game, we'll put some hints up around each branch. People are encouraged to ask questions of their leaders, or of anybody in the branch who might know the answer. By game time, they're pretty well prepared.

THE $1-MILLION INCENTIVE

During the second year of the program, we put out another incentive, just to encourage as many people as possible to come to the meetings. We told our employees: *If you come to 10 out of the 12 P&L meetings, you'll get an equal share of $1 million worth of PSS stock.* In 1997, 754 people were regular attendees, so each got $2,000-plus worth of stock (at today's value). That's how important we think it is for people in operations to take in all the information they need to run a tight ship.

ON THE SPOT

You know, there must be 100 different ways to encourage learning. For example, if you're a leader in a company, do you ever ask people questions? We do. We even have a book of questions about the business that we hope people will study. When I visit branches, I'll pull out my book and start tossing questions at people. Anybody who gives me the right answer gets $20. If they miss, they get nothing.

We call this process *On the Spot,* because it literally puts people on the spot. But it's just one more way of showing people how serious we are about learning the business. After all, if you're going to think and act like a CEO, you have to know what's going on. And people who know what's going on tend to keep the operational side of our business humming smoothly. Information is power. They have it, and they exercise it.

The Fifth Commandment: Open up your company. Make sure everybody sees and learns to understand all the information you can possibly give them. It's the only way to help people think and act like CEOs.

COMMANDMENT VI
Commit to Performance

It always amazes me how casual a lot of companies are toward
the one thing that determines their success: performance.

Sure, they have goals. They expect to see sales climb *x* percent. They want earnings growth of so much a quarter. Internally,
they have plans, budgets, and forecasts, and managers are
expected to meet them. If a company is publicly traded, its executives know that the stock will live or die by how well the company does compared to expectations. So it would seem that
performance measurements are not exactly ignored.

Look more closely, though, and you get a different picture.

The goals themselves, for example, are often plucked out of
thin air. Company executives look at last year's record. They
consider inflation. They tack on a couple of percentage points so
that it looks as if they have great hopes for the business. Presto:
There's our objective for the year. In most companies, the annual

objectives bear no relationship to long-term goals, because there aren't any long-term goals. Nor are they built on a solid foundation of information and discussion. The people who run plants and business units get their objectives (and their budgets) from on high. They're told what to do—but they don't really know where the growth is supposed to come from or how it's going to be realized.

Then, too, how many people actually *see* and *use* the annual objectives, plans, and budgets?

Usually, the only people in the know are senior managers, plant managers, and maybe department heads. It's their job to make sure their units hit the targets. But think for one minute about what happens when only a few people at the top have responsibility for goals. The natural response is this: Everybody else could care less. If sales reps don't make quota—hey, that's their problem, not customer service's or accounting's. If a plant isn't shipping what it's supposed to be shipping, blame the manager—but don't blame the production workers. It's not *their* job to worry about performance.

At PSS—indeed, at nearly any faster company these days— you'll find a wholly different attitude toward performance.

We take our commitment to performance very, very seriously—so seriously that we are regularly accused of being performance fanatics. Every year, we discuss and debate throughout the whole organization until we come up with solid, achievable goals. Everybody gets involved in the process. Everybody understands how one branch's objectives support the long-term goals of the company as a whole. Everybody understands what has to happen if the goals are to be realized.

And what's the result? The result is that people *commit* to the goals. We reinforce that commitment through our compensation system. And because we're an open-book company, every single person in a branch is aware of the goals and pitches in to help achieve them.

Sound appealing? Well, it's a lot of hard work. But it's the key to PSS's consistently high level of performance. Here's how we do it.

The Forecast

Every year, starting in January, we get on planes and begin traveling. The *we* here means John Sasen, Gene Dell, Dave Smith, Jim Stallings, and myself—the senior leaders of the company.

Most of our leaders pretty much grew up with PSS. Except John Sasen and Jim Stallings. I'm not sure John and Jim knew what they were getting in for when they joined us. John, for example, had spent most of his career with Becton Dickinson, a multi-billion-dollar manufacturer in our industry. Becton Dickinson is a well-respected company, and John had a reputation as one of the best executives in the business. But don't get him started on what life was like in the world of large corporations. When it came to doing up the year's plan, for example, he'd hear from the planning department on matters such as how many pages his plan should run and how many graphs it should contain. He'd write it up according to the specs. Then he'd have to go up before the strategic review committee to get his plan approved. Once it was approved, it was up to him and him alone to figure out how to communicate the plan through the departments that reported to him. What happened? "Most of the time," he'll tell you, "no one even knew what the plan was."

Anyway, John joined PSS in 1990. It was just about the only time we went outside our ranks for a major hire. We did it for one simple reason: There was no one in the PSS ranks who had the skills necessary to help run the size company we were becoming. I know that I've emphasized the grow-your-own, promote-from-within philosophy of leadership throughout this book. And I believe it firmly. On the other hand, if you grow as fast as we have, you may not have time to grow the leaders you need. At some point you may need to find someone who shares your values, gets excited about your goals, *and* can bring a career's worth of skills and experience to the business.

For us, that person was John Sasen. He started as vice president of sales and marketing, quickly moved up to become chief operating officer, and is now president and CEO of the PSS division of PSS/World Medical. I couldn't have asked for a better partner and coleader.

But let's get back to those airplanes. Like most big-company execs, John had done a good deal of traveling when he was at Becton Dickinson. Even so, I'm not sure he was prepared for his new responsibilities.

Our fiscal year ends in March. In the last quarter of the fiscal year—January, February, and March—John and I and the executive vice presidents visit every single branch, all over the country. We spend at least a day at each one. We talk with the leaders and the people there about how they're doing. And we agree on a forecast for the coming year.

Our approach to this process is pretty simple. Say inflation is running at four percent. We start by assuming that all the salespeople will increase their sales four percent, and everyone in the branch will get that much of a raise. But then we want to know what the branch can do beyond that. Where are the new opportunities? How much can we increase our sales of equipment? If we added a new sales rep, would he or she have enough business to write? This is where we get down into the nitty-gritty of a branch's business. We yell at each other. We go back and forth. But when we come up with a forecast for projected sales and earnings, we know exactly where those sales and earnings are going to come from.

Understand, we will never *tell* a branch how to make their goals. That's up to them. We want to see aggressive goals, and we want to know they're based on real assessments of where the new customers and new revenues are going to come from. But once a branch sets its goal, it's up to the branch to achieve it.

What this process gives us is a real forecast: a highly detailed, person-by-person projection of exactly what that branch is *committed to make happen* during the coming year. Individual salespeople have targets for gross revenues and gross margin. Each sales rep signs off on his or her forecast. The branch as a whole has a target for gross revenue and net earnings. The leaders of the branch commit to those targets.

Monitoring Performance

Next, we have a three-pronged approach to making sure the branch hits its goals.

Our *regional vice presidents* see the numbers of every branch they're responsible for every month. If one month's numbers miss the forecast, we'll want to know why. If two months' numbers miss, we'll begin pouring in resources. We'll analyze exactly where the shortfall was. We'll ask the branch's leaders how we can help. Maybe it's an individual rep who's having problems. Maybe we're facing new competitive pressures and need to figure out a tactical response.

In ordinary times at PSS, we flip-flop the usual chain of command. So long as a branch is making its numbers, regional VPs are in a *staff* relationship to the branch's leaders. Their job is to help out—to provide whatever support the leaders request. Should the numbers head south, though, the VP is now in a *line* relationship to the branch. The VP has the authority and the responsibility to do whatever needs doing to make things right.

Open-book management plays a critical role here as well. In a PSS branch, everybody knows what the goals are. Everybody sees how the branch is doing at those monthly P&L meetings. Each sales rep's numbers are right out where everybody can check them. Naturally, there's a good deal of peer pressure to make the goals. But more than that, the meetings are a forum for brainstorming and discussion about ways everybody can pitch in. Is the branch delivering the no-hassle service that PSS promises to every single customer? Does it have control of its inventory? Are there ways for other people at the branch to help out a struggling sales rep?

For a branch leader, missing the forecast is always a serious situation. But unlike at a lot of companies, it isn't a burden he or she has to bear alone. Because of our open-book approach, everyone at the branch can help analyze the problem and can pitch in to help solve it.

Finally, the *compensation system* keeps everybody focused on the forecast. We'll get to the details of the bonus plan in Chapter 15. For now, it's enough to say that sales reps aren't eligible for a bonus unless they hit their individual forecasts, and branch leaders don't get a bonus unless they hit their net-earnings targets. As you'll see, this is a *very* big incentive to make sure things stay on track. It reinforces our message about the importance of monitoring performance and hitting those forecasts.

In some cases, we'll also negotiate what we call a *high/low salary* for branch leaders. If you're a branch leader and you want a raise of 15 percent, maybe we'll give it to you—but only if you commit to a 15 percent improvement in your branch's earnings. If you fail to meet that goal, your salary drops back to its old level. That's another powerful incentive for hitting those numbers.

Is all this magic? I wish it were!

The fact is, PSS operates in a fiercely competitive industry. Our competition has the audacity to call on our customers every day, trying to steal our business. So, yes: There are times when our branches miss their revenue targets. There are some branches that don't make the margins we're shooting for, so their earnings suffer. Once in a while, we'll have a branch that loses money when it should be profitable.

But that's business.

If anything in this book has led you to believe that PSS has some kind of mystical, always-effective formula for success, forget it. People are people. They don't win every battle. They make mistakes. They slack off. Sometimes they're outsmarted or even outperformed by someone else. Even as dominant a team as the Chicago Bulls in their heyday didn't come out on top in every game. We have some great competitors, and we're not going to win every single time.

What we do have is a formula that encourages people to perform at the highest level they can. Ultimately you want to win—not every time, maybe, but much more often than you lose. You want to build up a high-performance organization, an organization in which people *care* about winning and *want* to win and *try very hard* to win all the time. Then you'll hit those targets—or better them!—most of the time. You'll create a company that will *never* settle for mediocre performance.

Frankly, I think that's where a lot of companies miss the boat. They settle. They throw up their hands and say, oh well, maybe next year will be better. They take it for granted that business has its ups and downs, that they'll have some good years and some not-so-good years, and that's life. Of course, it *is* life: Nobody wins all the time. But nobody has to settle, either. *You* don't have to settle. A faster company takes its performance goals seriously, and everybody in the company commits to those goals. It's the only way to ensure the kind of year-in, year-out performance a faster company needs to stay on top.

The Sixth Commandment: Commit to performance. Everyone in the organization needs to get involved in shaping the company's goals, in understanding them, in monitoring them—and in helping fix things if the company gets off track. (And a special thank-you here to Rick Schlosser, for introducing me to the concept of bottom-up forecasting.)

CHAPTER
13

COMMANDMENT VII
Pour It On!

In Chapter 4 I wrote about the importance of establishing a competitive edge. A *real* competitive edge. Some combination of product and service that you can provide to customers and that nobody else can.

That's a basic building block of a faster company, and if you can't establish that, then the rest of this book won't be worth much to you. But there's a fact about business that you have to remember, which is that the marketplace never holds still. So it's never enough just to establish your competitive edge and then sit back and relax. You have to push the envelope every day. You have to improve what you offer every year. You have to *widen* the gap between your company and the competition. You have to get in your competitors' faces and show the world that you can do things they can't.

In short, you have to pour it on. You can *never* rest on your laurels.

This seems obvious, right? But a lot of companies forget it.

Maybe they come up with a pathbreaking new product or service and figure that will let them dominate their marketplace forever. Remember Osborne Computer? That was the company that made the first portable computers. Granted, by today's standards, the computers were about as portable as your living-room TV. But at the time they were a real innovation, and they found a ready market. Osborne, unfortunately, grew too fast and wound up going broke. They were great on product development, not so great on the other basics of business.

Or maybe the company is number one in its marketplace, so it figures it can sort of relax. Not too long ago, Sears was the biggest general-merchandise retailer, and Kmart was the biggest discount house. Neither of them saw Wal-Mart coming until the upstart was breathing down their necks. It's a story that has been repeated in many industries.

But the real difficulty with this commandment goes beyond just remembering it.

The real difficulty lies in the fact that business battles are always taking place on several fronts at once. One competitor is attacking your territory. Another is learning how to deliver better service than you do. A third is making an alliance so that it has access to new capital. A fourth is wooing some of your key people. Any one of these competitive challenges may prove fatal to your business—so you have to counter them all. You have to attack on many fronts, and you have to be relentless on every one.

Is this really possible? The answer is yes, because faster companies know something that others have not yet learned: *Every victory makes the next one easier.* Every attack you mount in one area reinforces your attack in another area.

You need an overall objective, of course. You need people who can get the job done, and you need everything else we've talked about in previous chapters. But if you have all that, you *can* attack on all those fronts at once because you grow stronger every time you win. That's how companies come to dominate their competitors. That's how they stay on top year after year after year. Right now PSS is the number-one company in its industry. This chapter will tell you how we got there—and how we plan to stay there.

Opening Up New Territories

When we started, we were a tiny little company in Jacksonville, Florida. But pretty soon we heard about a few reps over in the Tampa/St. Petersburg area who wanted to join us. I went over, talked to them, and did a deal on the spot. Over the next few years we grew to half a dozen branches, all in Florida. Then we added a few more in other southeastern states.

Once we got our feet under us, though—and once we set that goal of becoming the first national physician-supply company— we began to expand with a vengeance.

For us, territorial expansion has always started with market analysis. We'd look for cities not too far away from our existing facilities and then examine who was serving physicians in that market. Was it crowded? Underserved? Were doctors dependent primarily on hospital-supply houses? Did any competitor have the capabilities we did? Sometimes we'd have a particular reason for expanding into an area, such as when we sent a sales rep into Beaumont, Texas. That was the home base of one of our toughest competitors, Taylor Medical. Taylor was making a lot of its profits close to home, and we wanted to attack the company right on its own turf.

Once we analyze a market, we'll explore the possibilities for an acquisition. Thanks to our sales of equity—$2 million venture capital in 1988 and equity from the public markets in 1994 and 1995—we've had money to spend. Our first acquisition was in New Orleans. Then we went to Mobile, Alabama, and to Chattanooga, Tennessee. By 1992 we had bought eight companies, and, of course, we've added dozens since then. Typically, we'll contact all the companies servicing physicians in the area and ask them if they want to sell. Most of them are small, family-owned businesses, with maybe 20 employees.

SUCCESSFUL ACQUISITIONS

The key to a successful acquisition is this: You have to *add value*.

In our case, adding value is pretty simple: We replace the old business model with our business model. Many of the companies we acquire aren't making a lot of money. They aren't growing. But we know we can grow nearly any medical-distribution company and make it profitable, because we know how to do things that our competitors don't. We introduce same-day service. We analyze the territory to make sure that the company has enough sales reps to cover all the physicians—and if it doesn't, we'll bring in some of our own. (Often, we'll end up with five times as many reps as the old company had.) We'll also teach the reps how to sell at higher margins—and the PSS reps we bring in demonstrate that, yes indeed, you *can* sell at higher margins.

Finally, we'll bring in a PSS leader and introduce our company's fast-paced, get-it-done, open-book culture. It takes a while for people in an acquired company to change, sure. In fact, a lot of them find our ways of doing things pretty hokey at first. It's amazing how people *can* change, though, when they see that new methods work better and can put more money in their pockets.

If I had my way, we'd expand entirely by acquisition. An acquisition is just a whole lot easier than a startup. The facilities are in place. The reps have well-established relationships with physicians. It doesn't take a lot of cash, because once you acquire the target company's assets, you can turn around and borrow against them. An acquired company, even one that's losing money, can be turned around and made profitable much more quickly than a startup.

The only problem with growth through acquisition is that you have to find a willing seller. For many years, that was pretty tough. Business for most of these companies was good, and they didn't want to sell out. So that was when we would take the startup route.

STARTUPS

Starting up is *hard*. Anybody who has done it will tell you how hard it is. But experience counts. We've started up 37 PSS branches over the years and have made every single one into a successful company. That kind of experience has taught us how to do a startup that knocks the socks off the competition.

The basis for a successful startup, of course, is a successful business model. That's what the rest of this book is about. Once your business model is in place, there are really only three keys to launching it in a new marketplace.

Key #1 is *speed*. You make the decision, commit the resources, and line up a leader. Then you move—*fast*. We've gone into a city and gotten a warehouse up and running literally over a weekend. Monday morning, our sales reps are out calling on physicians' offices.

Why so fast? Well, you don't want to squander time and money. You want to convey a sense of urgency to the troops. Mostly, though, you want to take the competition by surprise.

Surprise is a powerful weapon. Suppose, for example, that Joe Jones is running a successful medical-distribution company. He has learned to compete in his marketplace, and he is doing pretty well. All of a sudden, one day he notices these new trucks with PSS on the side. Boom—suddenly things don't look so bright! He has heard of PSS. He knows we can offer service that he can't. He knows we're going to be calling on *his* customers today, and tomorrow, and every day after that, with some of the most skillful, best-trained salespeople in the industry.

So what does Joe do? Most likely, he panics. He slashes prices. He gives his salespeople raises in hopes that they won't defect.

Before long, he isn't making money—and he hasn't even begun to learn to service his customers the way PSS can.

Competitors like Joe *hate* it when we turn up in their back-yards. And if they're caught by surprise, they hate it even more.

Key #2 is *persistence*. From our point of view, of course, it isn't so easy. We know those sales reps probably won't get a single sale the first day, or maybe even the first week. We know our trucks will be going out nearly empty for a short while, and only half full for a long while.

But you just have to ignore all that. The reps have to keep dropping in on their potential customers. Maybe there's something the doc's office needs right away—do they know that PSS can deliver the same day? Maybe they have something on back order from someone else—do they know that PSS has that in stock? Before long, the rep will get one order, and then another. Meanwhile, the trucks have to keep going out, every single day. When physicians and nurses start to experience our *same-day, no-hassle service*, many can't believe how they ever got along without it. That's when they make PSS their primary supplier. But it won't happen until every rep has called on every potential customer many times, and until every truck driver has delivered a lot of air along with our products.

Key #3 is *patience*—and a strong stomach.

It takes us between 15 and 18 months, on average, to get a new branch to the point where it's consistently making money. We have to set up and stock the warehouse. We have to get the trucks and bring them in. We have to pay the sales reps and operations people and leaders. The loss is generally about half a million dollars on an investment of up to $2 million—but it can be considerably more. We went into Chicago with a startup branch, for example, and because the territory was so big, we dropped 14 salespeople in there at the same time. That branch lost $800,000 before it turned profitable, but our leader, Matt never gave up. Today, we are a market leader in Chicago.

So starting up is a risky, stomach-churning challenge. On the other hand, if we had waited until we could grow through acquisition alone, we might still be waiting. As I said, you have to attack on many fronts simultaneously.

Grabbing Market Share

Once you get into a territory, it's you against everybody else— and you have to win more often than you lose. Your goal is to boost your share of the market every year. At PSS, our goal is to be number one in every market we operate in. We shoot for the top, and we expect to make it.

The key measurement here? It's a number known in the retail and distribution industries as *same-store sales*.

Same-store sales is just what it sounds like: a single branch's performance, tracked from month to month and year to year. If same-store sales are going up faster than the market as a whole, you know you're swiping market share from somebody else. In other industries you might be looking at the performance of a single plant or product line, but the idea is the same. Typically, same-store sales in our industry go up maybe 5 to 6 percent per year. PSS's same-store sales have risen an average of 20 percent a year—more than 3 times the industry average.

In short, we swipe serious market share in nearly every city we compete in.

How do we do it? Part of it gets back to what we talked about earlier. We think our sales reps are the most carefully selected, best-trained, hardest-working folks in the business. So we set high standards for them.

We want them to call on 20 to 30 customers a day, whereas most other companies expect only 20 calls max.

We expect them to *sell* those customers, not just to take orders.

We expect them to meet or beat their forecast.

And, of course, we always have those sales trainees waiting in reserve, so we don't miss a beat when a branch needs a new rep.

We also analyze our marketplace to figure out just how much business we can do. Some of our competitors get this process exactly backward. They hire a certain number of salespeople, then do whatever business those reps can bring in. We determine how much business is out there, then put enough reps on the street to make sure we get it.

We have one more ace up our sleeve, too: sales of equipment.

Traditionally, medical-supply houses didn't sell much equipment because doctors didn't buy much equipment. Medical tests and analyses were performed in hospitals or in separate labs. Recently, of course, all that has been changing. The technology in any number of areas has improved to a point where doctors, using new equipment, can perform many tests and analyses right in the office. I don't think anybody in the industry has been as aggressive as PSS about learning this new technology and explaining its benefits to doctors. We always make sure that our reps are up on the latest equipment and that they understand both the clinical and the financial benefits it can provide.

When you develop this kind of capability, good things happen. You sell a lot of equipment. Better still, manufacturers notice that you're selling a lot of equipment. They start to ask themselves whether they might be better off making an alliance with you. They could make the stuff, which they're good at. PSS could sell it, which we're good at. In the early 1990s, we began to have discussions with manufacturers along just these lines.

One example is Abbott Laboratories.

Abbott is one of the most highly respected manufacturers in the business. They produce a full line of diagnostic equipment with a lot of proprietary technology. They had been selling it themselves through their in-house sales force. We were competing against them with other manufacturers' products.

But the Abbott people were examining their options. As part

of the process, they hired a consulting firm to survey the customers who bought their products and competitive products. At the time, they weren't thinking of making any special deal with PSS, as opposed to other distributors. But when the survey came back, frankly, it blew them away. PSS was rated so high in its levels of service that they targeted us as a possible distributor.

So they called us, and over a three-month period we worked out a deal. It was a tough negotiation. We argued over the margins at which we would sell the equipment. We argued over exclusivity. But, finally, we came to terms. We would be the sole distributor for Abbott's full line of diagnostic products in physician offices with fewer than 25 physicians. They would buy a chunk of our stock. When we announced the deal to Wall Street, our stock went through the roof. Our successful relationship with Abbott has been a real win-win for both companies.

As it turned out, the Abbott deal was a harbinger of the future. Since then we have made exclusive arrangements with such companies as Hologic and Siemens. Market share? Ever since we got those exclusives, we've been *grabbing* market share. When a physician who wants a certain product *has* to come to you, you know your same-store sales are going to be growing. But it wouldn't have happened if we hadn't built the channel and the capabilities first.

Pushing the Envelope

When we started out, you'll remember, we offered our customers next-day service. That was just about unheard of at the time, and customers were flabbergasted when something they ordered on Monday turned up at the office on Tuesday. But that's a perfect example of a laurel you should not rest on. After all, there's nothing magic about next-day service; you just have to have the right systems in place. And there's nothing to stop a competitor from learning how to do it as well as PSS could.

So as quick as we could, we moved to same-day service. There's nothing magic there, either. Still, it ratchets the bar up another notch or two. Now a competitor has to have the technology to transmit orders electronically, as well as the systems to deliver them. It's that much harder and that much more expensive for anyone to copy us.

But we haven't exactly been resting on the laurel of same-day service, either. Once again, we've been moving the bar up a couple of notches.

For example, we're giving our customers direct access to our facilities through the Internet. They'll be able to dial in through our Web site and check our stocks, see the status of their back orders, and place new orders. Mind you, this is no ordinary Web site. They'll also have access through the site to reams of information about health care and physician practices. If they need to check the latest MSD sheets from OSHA, for example—these are safety-data documents relating to various chemicals—they can call up the appropriate screens and download or print out any of 88,000 different sheets.

Just as we've been pushing the technology envelope, we've also been diversifying into different combinations of price and value. When we started, we were the Mercedes of the industry. After our 1993 crisis, we learned to be more like a Chevrolet, with more competitive pricing. But the fact is, one size doesn't fit all. Some of our doctors love our Network Plus program, in which they agree to buy most of their supplies from PSS in return for lower prices. Others like our private-label products, which we can provide at a lower cost than name-brand products.

Once you establish yourself in one niche, there's nothing to prevent you from moving sideways into other niches, provided you always keep your focus. It's another way of expanding your share of the market.

The Advantages of Being Top Dog

When we merged with Taylor Medical in 1995, PSS became the largest physician-supply company in the United States. By early 1998, our Diagnostic Imaging division should be the largest X-ray sales-and-service company in the United States. Our long-term goal is simple: to be the biggest (and of course the best) health-care distribution company in the world. We want to be Numero Uno. On top. At the head of the line.

A lot of companies don't think they want to be number one. They think they're not big enough. They think somebody else is too well entrenched.

Personally, I say go for it. You don't have to be the biggest in the world, just the dominant player in your marketplace. Maybe you're only the biggest in your city. Maybe you dominate a particular niche. Look at a company such as the Goldhirsh Group, which publishes *Inc.* magazine. *Inc.* is hardly the biggest magazine around. It isn't even the biggest business magazine. But it utterly dominates the small business/growing company/entrepreneurship magazine market. And so it reaps the rewards of being number one, just as PSS does.

What are those rewards? I count three.

First, you notice a distinct shift in the balance of power in the marketplace. We used to have to court manufacturers, beg them to let us carry their lines. Now they're coming to us. When we negotiate prices, we have clout that we never used to have. If we ask for an exclusive, we're much more likely to get it than we would have been in the past. Any large company, of course, is likely to have clout in the marketplace. But the biggest one has more clout than anybody else.

Second, your competitors take you as a reference point. They set their prices in reference to yours. They judge their service levels in relation to yours. It's funny: They almost seem to take it for granted that you'll be on top, and that their job is to play Avis to your Hertz. I like that. It gives you a freedom of action that you don't have when you have to keep your eye on a bigger competitor.

Third, your customers take pride in doing business with you.

I have to say, I was a little reluctant to mention this advantage, because it can so easily backfire. Too many top-dog companies have decided that their customers should really be honored to do business with them, just because they're number one. And what happens? Suddenly they're number two—or worse.

If you maintain your position, though—if you continue, day in and day out, to deliver the best possible *value* to your customers—they really do want to do business with you. You're the biggest. You're the best. They know you'll be around and that you'll do what you say you're going to do. Think about it: If you have a package that (as they say) must absolutely, positively be there overnight, do you call anybody else but FedEx?

Being number one is great, just so long as you don't relax for a moment. It lets you expand your market even more.

All these moves, in fact, reinforce each other. When you expand your territory, you're making yourself better known and building up your power in the marketplace. When you grow your same-store sales, you're weakening your competitors by stealing their market shares. When you push the envelope by learning to do new things and deliver new value to the customer, you make it harder for anybody to overtake you.

It's a positive-feedback loop. But it requires that you pour it on. All day. Every day.

> *The Seventh Commandment: Attack! Grow! Take*
> *market share! Don't let up for a minute, even if it*
> *means attacking on several fronts at once. Get to be*
> *number one in your market—and stay there. (Thank*
> *you again to Jack Welch of General Electric: Being*
> *number one is a great strategy for long-term success.)*

COMMANDMENT VIII

Let Employees Fire the Boss

Every time you open up a business book these days, it seems, you see the word *empowerment*. Employees are empowered. Teams are empowered. At PSS, we believe in *real* empowerment—to the point where we expect employees to fire their bosses if they have to.

I'd better explain our thinking here, because it's easy to misunderstand.

First, this is not just a platitude on our part. It happens—and though it doesn't happen frequently, it does happen.

Second, the part that probably seems far out, crazy, and radical—the upside-down chain of command—isn't really so weird at all. It's just another element of a faster company. It helps you build a stronger, better organization.

Third, the truly radical part is the values we build into our organization—two key values in particular. Those values are what make the process work. If you can't accept them, you can't accept real empowerment.

Let's take these up one at a time, and maybe you'll understand why a faster company needs to put the employees in charge.

Getting Rid of the Boss

The call might come to the regional vice president or maybe to John Sasen. Often, it comes straight to me. Typically it will be from a veteran sales rep, but it might be from a truck driver or anybody else in a branch. We'll hear something like, "Pat, you better come in here. Several of us here don't think our leader is working out." When we get a call like that, John or I or the regional VP will drop everything and fly in to visit that branch. We'll sit down with the people, no leaders present, and ask them what's going on.

Occasionally, we don't even need a call. Not long ago, for example, I was visiting a midwestern branch to do the annual forecast. We started out with all the salespeople in one room, going over each person's numbers. They were quiet, hesitant. They didn't see how they could accomplish much next year. After about the third one, I stopped and said, folks, we need to take a break. Then I asked the leadership team to leave.

When the leaders had gone, the salespeople began to talk. They told me they weren't getting much direction. They didn't feel that the branch's leaders appreciated their work. They were unhappy, and they let me know it.

The fact was, the sales reps were being a little unfair in this instance. Before, they had an extraordinary leader, whom we recently promoted to run a bigger branch. Their new leader was young and inexperienced, and there was no way he could measure up to the last guy. But fair or not, the fact was that the leader and the salespeople weren't working well together. That would spell trouble for the branch, and we knew it.

For us, that's a pretty typical situation. Since we have been growing so fast, we're often promoting people into leadership roles before they're ready. Then, too, it's a tough job taking responsibility for a PSS branch. You have to be a real leader, not a manager. You can't just tell people what to do. You have to earn everybody's respect. And if you don't, you're out.

Of course, one of these sessions doesn't always result in the departure of the leader. Once in a while we convince the employees to give the leader a second chance. And there was one branch, in the southeast, that called us in so many times that we finally had to say, "Guys, we don't have anybody else; you're going to have to get by with the leaders you've got." The most common outcome, though, is that the leader ends up leaving. We assign a new leader to that branch, and we listen carefully to make sure he or she is working out.

Is It Really So Radical?

This idea about employees firing the bosses is another subject that doesn't exactly endear me to business audiences. Usually it's one of those monkeys-running-the-zoo moments. *Come on, Pat. You say that, but it doesn't really happen, does it?* When I give them examples of how it really does happen, people get a little upset. You can see the looks on their faces: Is this guy as nutty as he sounds?

But the fact is, this really isn't such a bizarre idea.

Think for a moment about the job of a leader. It's to make a branch (or a business unit, or a department, or whatever) *work*. Leaders are responsible for delivering value to the customer, whether it's an internal customer or an external one. They have to create the teamwork necessary to deliver that value. If leaders can't deliver, the *customers* will fire them. They'll quit buying. They'll complain to the leader's superiors. These days, every company hears about leaders or managers who aren't performing, because no company can afford a department or a unit that doesn't perform. So a leader's job is in jeopardy all the time. In that respect, PSS is no different from any company that takes performance seriously.

So what is different at PSS? Simple: We hear about nonperformance faster.

At most companies, after all, things have to get pretty bad before senior management hears about leaders who aren't doing their jobs. There's gossip. Maybe the numbers head south. But it's hard to get a fix on the problem, because employees rarely feel comfortable telling top managers the truth. So the response from corporate, typically, is to look for every problem except a nonperforming manager. Maybe the difficulty is in the marketplace. Maybe some employees are slacking off. The thinking runs: *We really don't want to fire Joe, do we? He's a nice guy, and he's probably doing the best he can. Besides, he says the problem doesn't have anything to do with him.*

At PSS, *the employees are the cops*, the truth-tellers. They know before anybody else does when a leader isn't working out. We encourage them—we expect them—to let us know, too. That way we can move quickly to fix a problem or get rid of a leader who's in the wrong job. It's one thing that makes PSS a faster company.

What Makes It Work?

By now, you've probably guessed what the real key to this process is. It's right there in the previous section. *At most companies, employees won't tell top management the truth.* They won't go over their bosses' heads. They're scared to, and with good reason. Bosses who learn that subordinates have gone over their heads usually reach for the ax.

At PSS, we have a cardinal rule, enshrined in our Top 20: *Always communicate without fear of retribution.*

That means that nobody *ever* will get in trouble at PSS for going over somebody else's head.

This was another lesson I learned early in my career. I was working with General Medical, in Atlanta, and I had been offered a chance to move from sales into management. But then the branch manager left, and a new one came in. His name was Bob, and he felt I was too young to manage. He put me right back in sales.

Even at that age, I wasn't going to take that. So I went over Bob's head. I went straight to the vice president of the company with a letter that said something like this: "Bob will probably fire me for writing this, but I don't care. I was given a leadership opportunity in this company, and it didn't work out. So I'll make you a deal. I know you're thinking of closing the branch in Columbus, Georgia. I'll go down there as manager for six months. If I can't turn it around, you won't have to fire me, because I'll quit."

The vice president, Jerry, actually liked the fact that I went over Bob's head. He did make me manager of the Columbus branch, and I was in fact able to turn it around. Trouble was, Bob was still my boss. And when salary review came around, guess what? No raise. For me, the handwriting was on the wall: I had crossed Bob, and he would never forget it. It wasn't long after that I left General Medical to take my next job, with Intermedco.

So when we started PSS, it was to be a cardinal rule: *no retribution.* We tell our employees that over and over. More important, we act on it. Nobody has ever been disciplined or fired for calling someone in the corporate offices.

We also build this principle into the way we do things, all the way to the top of the company. That's right: the top of the company.

Every year, we have what we call an Officers and Directors Retreat. We get together at a resort club and hold our formal meetings. But we also let down our hair. *Way* down. We play PSS *Jeopardy!*—and there we are, the officers and directors of a billion-dollar publicly traded company, climbing on tables and screaming out answers, all in hopes of winning a PSS baseball cap. We play golf—and there we are again, out on the fairway, playing a tournament according to some of the nuttiest rules ever invented. (Sample: "Winners win cash but must make a donation to the Virginia Home for Boys. The team that includes Pat Kelly automatically wins.") At night, we'll have a barbecue or a luau.

Fun, right? But there's a very serious purpose. I want all PSS's officers to know all of PSS's directors personally. I want them to feel comfortable with one another. I want them to call each other if they ever think that I am messing up as CEO. The board, as a group, is my superior. And I want people to feel they can go over *my* head as easily as a branch's employees can go over their leader's head.

There's one other value that makes it all work: the *soft landing*. You've read about this in earlier chapters. If someone at PSS is promoted to a new job and doesn't work out in that job, he or she can always go back to the old job, or to a different job entirely. We don't bounce people out of PSS for taking on a new challenge and failing. This is important: After all, if firing the boss means he's going to lose his livelihood, most employees would naturally be reluctant to take action. At PSS, they know the boss will get a soft landing, and the chance to try again. So they don't hesitate to take action when it's appropriate to do so.

By the way, most of our leaders who failed are leaders again today. Some are even officers of the corporation. They learned from their mistakes and became better leaders.

The Eighth Commandment: Put the employees in charge. Expect them to fire leaders who aren't working out. You'll uncover problems a whole lot faster this way than if you wait for your customers to tell you. Fact is, employees will ultimately fire bad leaders anyway, because they won't perform for them. Why go through the agony?

COMMANDMENT IX
Make a *Lot* of Millionaires

This chapter is about money. Compensation. How you pay people, and how much, and why.

Compensation is always a touchy subject. Everybody in business has an opinion about how much he or she ought to be paid. Every business owner and corporate executive has an opinion about how much the company ought to be paying. These two opinions rarely coincide, so money becomes a bone of contention. People quit over money. Unions go on strike over money. Money is the main item on the agenda in every annual review, every budget meeting, and every discussion about promotion.

No wonder so many companies simply throw up their hands, hire a compensation consultant to design a system, and then hope that will be the end of the debate. Of course, it never is.

The compensation issue also gets companies in trouble faster than almost anything else.

Sometimes companies pay people too much. Think of the workers at the big steel companies 20 years ago, for example. They made twice what the average U.S. worker made—and then wondered why their jobs evaporated in the face of competition from the Japanese and the new minimills. Think of the organization men (and organization women) who used to inhabit the bloated bureaucracies of companies such as General Motors and IBM. They had nice salaries, nice perks, nice benefits—until their employers began bleeding red ink. Then they, too, were out on the street.

And sometimes companies pay people too little.

I felt Intermedco was paying me too little, for example, that year that I helped bring the company into profitability and got no raise.

And my pal Gene Dell, the PSS veteran whom you met earlier in this book, will tell you that he wasn't too happy with his last employers, either. He was a great salesman, and he'd do things like double the sales of the small companies he worked for. Then he'd be lucky to get a five percent raise. After all, you wouldn't want a young sales rep to be making more than the vice president, would you?

So companies lose their good people by not paying them enough. In Intermedco's case—and in many, many similar situations—they not only lost an experienced leader, they spawned their own competition.

These days, there's yet another dimension to the compensation puzzle.

Over the last several years, it has become common for companies to add all kinds of variable compensation to their employees' base pay. They set up stock-ownership plans. They give out options. They launch gain-sharing and other bonus systems. It used to be that only the people at the top were eligible for goodies like these. Today, more and more companies are extending variable-comp incentives throughout the organization.

We at PSS have had to grapple with our pay system just like

any company. We don't have all the answers. The specifics of our system may or may not work for you, depending on things like your company's history and what the expectations are in your industry.

What we do have, though, is a pretty clear *philosophy* of compensation. And that should work for you every bit as well as it works for us. The basic idea is simple. We want people to earn what they make—and then to get every penny of what they earn. When our company does well, we want our people to do well. And when our people do well, we want the company to do well.

In short, we want to *align* the interests of the company and its employees. That way, money isn't always a bone of contention. If people want more, they know they have to help the company make more money. And if they do, we make sure that they get more.

Here's how we put these ideas into practice.

Pay for Performance

The phrase *pay for performance* is almost a buzzword these days. But does your company really reward performance? Or does it do things like this?

- Put a cap on salespeople's commissions.

- Issue across-the-board raise policies, regardless of business-unit results.

- Pay bonuses even when the company (or a business unit) doesn't reach its goals.

If it does any of these things, it isn't really paying for performance.

See, *performance* in business doesn't mean trying hard. It means getting the job done. It means achieving your goals. It means making money. Performance happens (or not) at the level of individuals and teams, and only later at the company level. Salespeople do or do not meet their forecast. A branch does or does not make its profit goals. A staff department does or does not achieve its productivity targets. Only when people are performing can the company perform.

At PSS, performance sets the baseline for all our discussions about money.

If a branch hits certain targets, its people get bonuses. If it doesn't, they don't.

If sales reps hit their forecasts, they're eligible for a share of that bonus. If they don't, they aren't. (More on our bonus system later in this chapter.)

If a branch or a region increases its profits ten percent, then we'd be glad to talk to the branch or regional leaders about a ten-percent raise. But if revenues and profits are flat, we're really not interested in hearing how hard everybody is working and how much they deserve a raise.

If people at PSS are performing, there's *never* a cap on what they can earn. There's no ceiling, for example, on salespeople's commissions. That's why some of our top reps earn upwards of $200,000 a year. There's no maximum on the bonuses we pay to our branch leaders and branch employees. If they can boost profits, they can boost their bonuses.

I like to point to the example of one of our southern branches, which often finishes at the top of our list in terms of performance. Last time I looked, this branch had a 40 percent share of the market. They had recorded a 34-percent gross profit and 11-percent pretax net. Those are some great numbers! By turning in that kind of performance, the branch's leaders added $40,000 or $50,000 to their annual income. The warehouse workers, truck drivers, and every other employee in the branch got a bonus amounting to nearly $10,000 apiece. To someone who would otherwise make maybe $20,000 a year, that's a nice piece of change. Do you see why we have such motivated employees?

An Open-Book Bonus System

A lot of companies pay bonuses, but very few pay them effectively. Employees don't know what they have to do to earn a bonus. The books aren't open, so they don't know how the company is performing. If people get a bonus, they're happy—but they don't really understand what they did to deserve it. If they don't get a bonus, they're not so happy. In that case, they generally figure that management doesn't know what it's doing or that it's just pocketing the profits. (They may be right.)

At PSS, we turn the whole bonus program into a game. Everybody plays. Everybody can win. And everybody knows how they're doing, month by month, so they can figure out how to get better.

The details of the game often vary from year to year, just to keep it interesting. But here's what the program looked like in 1997.

We called the program *Field of Dreams '97*. Everybody in PSS got a short, simple description of how it worked. The description spelled out the guidelines—the rules of the game.

Some of these rules are the kind of thing you find in any bonus program. The payout schedule, for instance: We pay every six months, at midyear and year-end. And eligibility: You have to be employed at PSS six months prior to payout to be eligible for a bonus.

But other rules are there specifically to reinforce our system. Sales reps don't get a share of their branch's bonus unless they achieve their gross-profit forecast. Operations people must attend 10 out of the 12 PSS Challenge meetings during the year. You've seen in earlier chapters how important things like the forecast and the Challenge meetings are to the way we operate. The bonus rules reinforce the message.

The bonus pool itself grows according to whether the branch hits a series of targets. Because we use a baseball theme, we call each target a *base*—and, just as in baseball, you have to reach first base before you can reach second base. If you hit all four targets, you get a home run and earn the biggest possible bonus.

So here are the bases:

First base   is five-percent net operating profit. If a branch hits that five percent, the bonus gate is open. Anything less and we don't feel the people in the branch have earned a bonus. Every branch has to return at least five percent of sales to the shareholders before we pay anything extra.

Second base   is hitting your earnings forecast. If you earn five-percent net operating profit but you forecast six percent, you only hit a single. (In practice, however, nearly every branch that hits a single also hits a double.)

Third base   is maintaining asset days less than 90. *Asset days*, as an accountant will tell you, measure two things: how well you're managing your inventory and how well you're managing your receivables. Our receivables have historically run about 50 days of sales and our inventory about 40 days cost of sales. We measure them both, and we expect the combined total to be under 90 days.

A *home run*   is meeting all those targets *plus* profits at least two percentage points better than your forecast. If a branch forecasts net profits of six percent and hits eight percent, it has hit a homer.

Every base you reach puts more money into the bonus pool. A branch that reaches first base gets a nickel of every profit dollar over and above that five-percent minimum. Say, for example, that a branch's sales are $10 million and net profit is $900,000. Since the net profit is $400,000 above the 5 percent cutoff, $20,000 goes into the bonus pool.

Second base adds another nickel to the pool. If the earnings forecast is exceeded, another $20,000 goes toward bonuses.

Third base adds yet another nickel. So long as the branch's

asset days are below 90, another $20,000 goes into the pool, bringing the total to $60,000.

And a home run adds one final nickel. So long as net profits are 2 percentage points above forecast profits, the pool grows by yet another $20,000.

Each target reinforces the others, because if you don't hit one, you have to stop at the previous base. A branch that had all the same numbers except asset days over 90, for instance, would wind up with only a double—and with only half as much in the bonus pool as the branch in our example. But if you hit a homer, then 20 cents out of every profit dollar over 5 percent flows right back to the employees' pockets.

This is a powerful system! Through this system, the people at a successful branch can put thousands of additional dollars into their pockets every year. Because the pool is divided up equally, it gives lower-paid people even more of an incentive—and it reinforces the message that everybody counts, that we all sink or swim together.

Moreover, once people understand the bonus, it's almost as if the branch is on cruise control. They watch sales and profits. They watch the forecast. They even watch asset days. If there's a problem, they solve it together. Here's how Dave Smith, our CFO, described this day-in, day-out monitoring process in an interview with Dr. Tom Barton, a professor at the University of North Florida. I think it captures perfectly the flavor of the discussion at PSS branches.

Let's say (Smith begins) that interest expense at a branch is too high because the branch has too much inventory. People begin analyzing the problem:

Well, why do we have too much inventory in stock? It could be a lot of reasons. One, purchasing isn't quite up to speed, or salespeople have asked us to bring in products that aren't moving. You've got to get the salespeople to move those products out so that it leaves room for the right number of inventory days. Or we brought a product in that everybody says was going to sell, and it hasn't sold. We need to do a sales program to get rid of it, or we need to start calling manufacturers to return the product.

Anyway, the team comes up with an answer that solves *their problem*. It's not corporate coming to the team and saying, "Get your interest cost down." The team itself comes up with an answer because they're going to be compensated on their performance to this budget.

Eventually, Smith continues,

they get down to the *Nth* degree of detail: how much they pay each other, how much gasoline they're using per truck, where they're spending money in their branch. Are they spending too much on freight or electricity or telephone? . . . Do we have a territory that's not producing, and do we need to talk to that person and get them producing? It's almost like an internal police force. They talk to their own people and say, "Look, you're not pulling your weight in this area. You've got to help us out here." . . . They can also create entrepreneurial solutions. They can make their job easier and more efficient and create more profit on the bottom line if they know that their job or area is costing so much, and if it's over or under budget.

That kind of discussion just wouldn't take place if it weren't for the bonus system. The bonus helps keep us all focused on performance.

Stock Ownership

We've already talked about employee ownership in this book. I said it's a no-brainer, and I believe it. A company with employee owners has three big advantages over the competition.

First, owners have an interest in the long-term success of the business, not just in this year's profits.

As any businessperson knows, long-term success sometimes requires short-term sacrifice. When we reoriented our business in 1993, for example, we took hits on our margins. Earnings suffered. Salespeople lost commissions. Not many branches got a bonus. But it was worth it in the long term, because it enabled us to get back on the growth path. Before long, the stock value was rising again—and our employee shareholders could see that all the pain had been worth it.

Second, stock ownership ties employees to the company—and vice versa.

Like a lot of industries these days, ours is a high-turnover business. Our sales reps are always being wooed by the competition. Our good operations people have plenty of other opportunities, too, often at companies that can afford higher base wages than we can. Stock ownership encourages all our people to stick around for the long term. That's good for PSS, because people are the only asset we can't easily replace. And it's good for our employees, because they can see that nest egg of stock growing every year.

Third, stock ownership brings excitement to business. After all, that's how people make real money.

It's hard to get rich on a salary. It's hard to get rich even on salary and bonus. Sure, maybe you can do it if you're the CEO of a giant corporation or if you're a fancy New York lawyer pulling down a million dollars a year. But most people earn more modest amounts, and nearly all of us spend what we earn. A truck driver making $30,000 in salary and bonus isn't so different in this respect from a sales rep or branch leader making $100,000. They may have different life styles. But neither one is going to be piling up big bucks in the bank.

When you own stock, though, something amazing happens: Suddenly, you can amass wealth well beyond what you can earn in wages or salary.

And when you own stock in a growth company, that stock can appreciate *fast*. I'm writing this book in 1997, just a little more than three years after we went public. In that time, the value of a PSS share has grown fivefold.

The upshot? Depending on the stock price, we have anywhere from 100 to 200 millionaires among PSS employees and former employees. And we have many, many more employees who are rapidly accumulating healthy six-figure portfolios. Many of these people don't have fancy jobs. They may not have attended college. But through stock ownership, they all can earn real money.

We want all of our employees to own stock, so we set up a lot of mechanisms to encourage it. There's a formal Employee Stock Ownership Plan (ESOP), which includes all employees with one year of service. The ESOP is our single biggest shareholder, and we allocate shares to each individual's ESOP account every year. There's also an individual stock-purchase plan, which allows people to buy shares as individuals through payroll deductions. And there are generous awards of stock options: For example, every employee with five years' service may get a grant of options.

Stock ownership is just like anything else, though: People have to learn its value. We make a point of teaching people about stock and showing them how they can save for the future by buying shares. We encourage people to track the price every day and to understand why it moves up and down the way it does. We schedule shareholders meetings so that as many employees as possible can attend. Over time, of course, people build up bigger and bigger nest eggs, and the word spreads from one employee to another: *This is where the money is.* Stock ownership is one key part of a compensation system that gets us all pulling in the same direction, working toward the same ends: the success of the business, and the success of each other.

The Ninth Commandment: Share the wealth!
Set up pay systems that encourage and reward
performance. Make every employee a shareholder,
so that everyone is pursuing the same goals.

COMMANDMENT X

Out with Bureaucracy!

If you want to send a memo at PSS, here's how you do it. You wait until the last day of the month. Then you drink a lot of coffee and stay up late. At precisely 12:01 A.M. on the first day of the month, you fax your memo to all our branches.

See, we have a rule. Everybody is required to read the first memo they get each month. After that, they can do anything they want with them. Wad them up and fire a jump shot at the wastebasket. Make them into paper airplanes and shoot them across the warehouse.

As you maybe guessed, this is something I have strong feelings about. I'm scared to death of memos. I'm scared to death of putting things down on paper.

Why? Because I've seen bad things happen from too much paper.

Once you start writing everything down, a kind of corporate

arthritis begins to set in. Suddenly, the organization that moved so fast and stayed so flexible has *rules* and *regulations* and *procedures*. Suddenly, the company that was growing like gangbusters is *maturing* and *settling in*. Suddenly, the company that was *nutty* is—well, it's just like every other company. It has policy manuals and rulebooks. It has standard operating procedures. And it has memos.

Friend, this is not going to happen as long as I am running our company. And I urge you not to let it happen at your organization, either.

I like to say I have a full-time job as CEO of this billion-dollar enterprise known as PSS/World Medical: to continue to root out bureaucracy.

So far, it's working. PSS has no policy manual. We have almost no written rules and regulations. Thanks to the memo rule, we don't have a helluva lot of written communication.

Of course, we comply with the law. We don't discriminate on the basis of race or religion or age or gender. We won't tolerate sexual harrassment. To us, all that is just a matter of good sense and treating people right. But it's also the law of the land, and you have to make sure everyone knows you abide by the law. So we did up a cute poster, with little cartoon figures representing John Sasen and me explaining these policies, and we put it up in every branch. That's our written statement.

Otherwise, we don't have policies. Sick leave? That's a matter for each branch to decide. Vacation time? Same. I can't see sitting in corporate headquarters in Jacksonville and worrying about whether a truck driver in Denver is entitled to three more vacation days. Our people are adults. They know the job that has to be done, and they know they're responsible for getting it done. So they can make their own policies and schedule their own time.

Of course, we are now a big company, with branches all over the United States and (increasingly) in Europe. We have to have some way of making sure we're all on the same page, delivering the same level of service, and meeting our customers' expectations in the same way. And we do; we just don't do it with written rules and memos and all the other trappings of bureaucracy.

This chapter tells you how—first our general approach and then a handy little tool for keeping everyone on the same page and having a good time doing it.

Culture and Communication

If you read about business regularly, you've heard of the famous "H-P way" at Hewlett-Packard. You've read about the hard-driving environment at Intel and the zany atmosphere at Southwest Airlines. The best companies invariably have a distinct (and distinctive) culture. They have a way of doing things that everyone seems to understand and take for granted.

PSS is no exception. As you've seen in this book, we have unusual ways of doing things. We tell people over and over what they are, through a dozen different methods.

We put our key values, for example, onto that Top 20 card that every PSS employee carries in his or her wallet. We refer to it a lot. People know from the Top 20 that (for example) we *strive to promote from within*, that we want people to *suggest and encourage better ways of doing things*, and that we want people to *treat all company assets as if they owned them*. (Another one of the Top 20: *Minimize paperwork and memos.*)

We teach new sales reps how PSS works, and if they go on to become leaders, we teach them more. All that training at PSS University and later during Creativity Week helps people understand how we do things. Nobody comes out of that training without understanding the importance of same-day, no-hassle service. Sales reps all learn to manage their accounts in the same way. Leaders learn how PSS branches all over the country operate.

We also get up in front of employees regularly. All the senior leaders of the company make a point of visiting branches and talking to our employees. The regional leaders drop in on all their branches regularly. Employees come to regional and even national meetings. Every time we talk to them, we'll discuss some part of PSS's culture.

Many employees at PSS move from branch to branch, and when someone is promoted into a leadership role it's likely to be at a new branch. That helps spread the culture, too.

And as you've probably noticed by now, we have dozens of different slogans and sayings. They get repeated so often that they're hard to escape. For example, I'd bet there's scarcely a single person among our thousands of employees who doesn't know what a *soft landing* means.

As you can see, it's not communication that I'm against. Quite the contrary: Every company needs continuing communication with its people, and the bigger you get the more you need it. But I want people communicating face to face as much as possible, or at least talking on the phone. There's a big difference between written and spoken communication! Talking is two-way. People ask questions until they understand what you're driving at. Writing is one-way. Once you write things down, it's as if the words are set in stone. People stop thinking for themselves and start referring to the manual or the memos.

I've seen that happen with the written word, and I hate it. For example, I once went to a branch just as they were about to take their physical inventory. And I heard about a customer that wasn't getting the product she needed.

So I asked one of the employees, "Why aren't you shipping this?"

"I can't," he said. "I got a memo that says I can't." And he showed me a memo that said you couldn't ship product during the three days prior to inventory.

Well, there was a reason for that memo. We don't want product in transit between our own branches during inventory. But *of course* we can ship to a customer—how else can we meet the customer's needs? And the employee hadn't stopped to think about that, because the memo failed to explain it.

That day, I ripped that memo off the wall. I encourage other leaders in the company to rip memos off the wall, too. We're only human, so people do continue to send out memos, even after midnight on the first of the month. But I want to make it crystal clear to everyone in our company: You don't have to read them. And you certainly shouldn't treat them as if they were laying down the law.

The Blue Ribbon Tour

As this book went to press, we had 106 branches. By the time you read it, the number will have grown. Every branch is responsible for its own business, which means that the people leading the branch have to be entrepreneurially minded. And we have no policy manual setting out the rules and regulations.

So I'm sure you're thinking: Culture or no culture, communication or no communication, you've got to have 106 people running off in 106 directions. Heck, how do you make sure the trucks are even painted the same colors, let alone ensure that every branch offers the same level of service to customers?

The fact is, we do. You could walk into any one of our branches and it would look, feel, and operate almost exactly like all the others. We need that kind of consistency and uniformity because we're a national company and we have built a national reputation on doing things in a certain way. It's our business model, and we don't really want local leaders experimenting with business models of their own.

So how do we ensure that everybody's following it? The key is a handy, home-grown management technique we call the *Blue Ribbon tour*.

Twice a year, one of PSS's top leaders shows up at every single branch. Unannounced. It might be 7:30 in the morning or 4:00 in the afternoon or any time in between. "Blue Ribbon time!" he'll say as he walks in the door. For years, I did all the Blue Ribbons myself. As we've grown larger, I've shared the duties with John Sasen, Dave Smith, Gene Dell, and Jim Stallings.

The Blue Ribbon is an inspection. And what an inspection! We have a book with 100 points in it detailing the way we want every branch to look and how we want every branch to operate. We'll have the book in hand and we'll walk around, observing and listening, checking what they pass and fail on:

- Are the trucks clean?
- Are there refreshments available for guests?
- Is there a map showing all of PSS's locations?
- Are truck maintenance logs maintained?
- Is there a Wall of Fame celebrating employee accomplishments?
- Is the phone answered in three rings or less?

The questions go on and on. All told, the inspection usually takes between three and four hours. Every question is yes or no, so the branch will wind up with a score: so many points out of a possible 100. Of course, a Blue Ribbon visit isn't all checking the books. We talk to employees. We answer questions (and hand out $2 bills to everyone who asks one). We do On the Spot quizzes and pass out $20 bills to people who get the answers right. Still, everybody knows that they're being inspected. And they *really* want to know how they scored.

I can guess what you're thinking: At some companies, this kind of inspection would be a horrendous experience. A visit from Big Brother. And you're right.

At PSS, it's a little different. When people hear there's a Blue Ribbon on, they're whooping and hollering. They're running around making sure the wastebaskets are empty and there's toilet paper in the bathroom. What's at stake here, you see, isn't just a bland seal of approval from some corporate muckety-muck, it's real money. Not to mention bragging rights. The branch that scores highest on the Blue Ribbon gets $3,000 per employee. The second-place branch gets $2,000 per employee, the third-place branch $1,500 and so on, all the way down to $500 per employee for the tenth-place branch.

And the losing branches—all the rest—have to pay!

So, this isn't some military-style inspection greeted by fear and trembling. It's a game. The branches are competitors. The people in our branches take pride in keeping their facilities ready for a Blue Ribbon at all times. They take enormous pride in winning, and in mentioning the fact that they won to their friends in other branches.

At PSS, we believe there are a lot of ways to accomplish the same end. Sure, a company as big as ours has to have consistency and uniformity. But we don't have to have a bunch of written rules and regulations. We don't have to be issuing memos. We don't want to drown in a sea of paperwork, and we don't want to set up a bureaucracy. Instead, we'll figure out fun, face-to-face ways of achieving the kind of consistency we need to have. The Blue Ribbon is a perfect example.

> *The Tenth Commandment: Root out bureaucracy. Don't tolerate unnecessary paperwork. Abolish memos. And be creative: Figure out ways to get everybody on the same page and have a good time while you're doing it. Heck, start your own Blue Ribbon tour. (It isn't patented.)*

CHAPTER 17

COMMANDMENT XI

Have Fun

This commandment is short and sweet. The title says it all. Have a good time. Have fun.

I know: A lot of people don't believe that fun belongs in business. Business is a serious matter. It's work. I wish I could give all these people a Bronx cheer, but it's hard to do on paper.

We at PSS take our business seriously. We have to. We're providing physicians with the tools and materials they need to safeguard their patients' health. It's hardly an obligation that you'd want to take lightly. We treat our business responsibilities with equal seriousness. We live and die on same-day service. We watch our margins like hawks. We put those forecasts up on the wall, and we expect to make them. We're a high-performance company. There's about as much slack in our operations as in a U.S. Marine's jaw.

But can't you do all that and have fun, too? Do you really want to spend 8 or 10 hours a day, 5 days a week, 50 weeks a year with the same people and not enjoy yourself? We sure don't. Life is too short.

Of course, I've seen how some companies try to have fun. They have an annual picnic, with a few games and an awkward speech by the CEO. They have a Christmas party where everyone gets sloshed. And that's about it.

If you really want to have fun in your company, you have to have fun all the time. You have to set aside regular times to get together and enjoy yourself. You have to spend a little money. You have to encourage people to get together on their own time and get to know each other. It isn't so hard! In fact, pretty soon people will expect to have a good time with their workmates and will come up with ideas of their own as to how to do it. But here are a few to get you started.

Kelly Appreciation Day

Once every three months, we get everybody at corporate headquarters together and we go somewhere. Usually it's a surprise, announced the night before. One time we took everyone to the beach, where we had a surfing instructor and surfboards waiting. We took them to that alligator farm I mentioned earlier, and on the way we told them they'd have to wrestle a gator. We've put everyone on a plane and gone down to Key West to eat at a good restaurant and watch the sun set over the Gulf of Mexico. Sometimes we'll just throw a party at my house—and at the party we'll have special events, such as a drawing for an all-expenses-paid trip to Hawaii or a haunted house on Halloween for our employees' families.

The Challenge Game

I wrote about our Challenge games and monthly P&L meetings earlier, in Chapter 11. There, the context was serious: It's how we teach people about our business. But those meetings are a great way for everybody in a branch to get together and have fun.

For one thing, we always hold them at a fun place, like an amusement park or a bowling alley. We'll get dinner for everybody. When the meeting's over, people can go out and have a good time. Then, too, the Challenge games themselves aren't exactly quiet and peaceful. People yell out the answers, hoot and holler, carry on.

In fact, if you're ever at a business conference, check the agenda to see if anyone from PSS is doing a presentation using one of our games. You'll get a flavor of how we do things—and I guarantee you, you won't mistake our presentation for anyone else's. At the last Inc. 500 conference, for example, you'd have walked in to see balloons all over the place, boxes of Cracker Jacks (the topic was, "How to Create and Train a Crackerjack Sales Force"), and PSS blankets to be handed out as prizes. Up front, Marty Ellis and Becky Witt were leading the whole group in a game of *PSS Jeopardy!*—and people who had never before heard of PSS were suddenly climbing all over each other to take a shot at the answers. It's a little more fun than the average conference presentation.

Employee Picnics

Our annual picnics aren't half-day affairs at a local park. Instead, what we'll do is hold them over a weekend, typically near a theme park. They're organized by region, so employees don't have too far to travel. Most of the employees will drive up early Saturday morning. We'll have some meetings in the morning, give everybody lunch, and in the afternoon we'll hold our volleyball tournament. That evening, we'll buy people dinner and put them up in a hotel. Sunday, they're free to go out with their families and have a good time—at PSS's expense.

I have to say a word about that volleyball tournament. Volleyball is *big* at PSS, and we're a competitive bunch. The branches organize teams and practice regularly. They'll come to the picnics complete with T-shirts and organized cheering sections. If your branch wins the tournament, you're entitled to some serious bragging rights. (It has even been said that recruits who are six-three and have played volleyball in college have a much better chance of being hired than anyone else, but I'm *sure* that's not true.)

Annual Sales Meetings

Our annual sales meetings are over the top. There's no other word for it.

The meetings last four days. There's plenty of serious stuff. We bring in all our sales reps and their spouses, along with all the leadership of the company. We'll invite our top 30 vendors and spend a lot of time with them, learning about their new products. We have formal training programs and leadership seminars. The day starts at 7:00 A.M. It's work, no doubt about it.

On the other hand, we have a *very* good time.

In the evenings, for example, we'll have skits and parties, plus what I call my annual soapbox speech. It's kind of a state-of-the-union speech, but it isn't much like the real one. Last year I dressed up like Gen. Tony McAuliffe, the World War II commander who, when told that the Germans were expecting him to surrender at the Battle of the Bulge, replied with a famous answer: "Nuts!" My speech developed the theme. It's a nutty world we live in. We as a company had to be nutty to compete in it. Every punch line—"Nuts!"—brought people to their feet. Unfortunately, someone had given them bags of peanuts—which, of course, they proceeded to throw at the speaker and each other. A good time was had by all. And nobody was hospitalized from a ricocheted peanut.

To cap off the meeting, we'll do something really special. One year we rented Six Flags Over Texas, the amusement park. The whole thing. The next year we rented Stone Mountain Park, in

Atlanta. The park put on a laser show for us, complete with PSS's name projected onto the side of a mountain.

Little Things

When it comes to fun, little things mean a lot.

Maybe a branch will have an informal get-together at lunchtime, for example. The leaders will spring for pizza or sandwiches. They'll go outdoors and chat. Weekends, a leader might have people over to his or her house for a barbecue.

Often, regional leaders will get their new sales reps together for a weekend of good times. Charlie Alvarez, who runs our northeastern division, sponsors what he calls Camp Chico. One weekend, it seems, they managed to play touch football, basketball, volleyball, *and* kickball.

And even that Officers and Directors Retreat I mentioned in Chapter 14 is pretty wild. You wouldn't expect a bunch of middle-aged businesspeople, academics, and lawyers to enjoy themselves so much over things like *PSS Jeopardy!* and a zany golf tournament. But they do.

Having a good time at work is in many ways its own reward. You grow closer to your colleagues, establish better relationships with them. You make friends. You look forward to going in every morning. Your branch becomes a great place to work.

Fun also has its business payoffs. Once people have been with us for a while—once they've grown accustomed to our way of doing things—we scarcely lose anybody. People don't leave. Why would they? Not only are they making a lot of money, they're having too good a time. They *like* PSS and the people they work with. They're part of the family.

Ultimately, it all gets back to that slogan that I've repeated more than once in this book: *People are a faster company's only real asset.*

I don't mean by this only that you can go out and rent new

warehouses, buy new inventory, and get new trucks. Of course you can—but you can go out and hire new people, too. In theory.

But what makes people different from trucks and warehouses is what they carry around in their heads. The knowledge. The experience. The feelings about the company, and about each other. The commitment to do whatever it takes to satisfy the customer.

You can't hire people who come with those traits. You have to grow them and you have to keep them. In part, you do that by helping them realize their financial goals.

But you also do it by making it possible for them to have a good time. To feel great about what they do and the people they do it with. That's a feeling you can create—and that you can't buy.

The Eleventh Commandment is simplicity itself: Have fun. If people in your organization aren't enjoying themselves, you'll never have a faster company.

CONCLUSION

The Paradoxes of the Marketplace

So, there you are. Four building blocks. Eleven commandments. Building a company isn't like preparing a meal, of course, and a business book isn't a cookbook. So I can't give you step-by-step directions. But I hope I have told you what we at PSS think is important about creating a fast-growth, high-performance organization. And I hope I have showed you what we have learned in the 15 years we have spent building this nutty, home-grown, billion-dollar business known as PSS/World Medical.

Right now I want to come back to the idea of why it's worth creating a faster company. That's your objective, after all. That's the business payoff. If you take the ideas in this book, adapt them to your own situation, and then begin to apply them, you'll be on the way to building a company that is uniquely suited to today's environment. A company that cuts through the paradoxes and seeming contradictions of this turbulent marketplace we all have to work in. A company that can literally do things other companies can't.

What are those things? I count four. For ordinary companies, they're paradoxes, which means something to get tangled up in. They're potholes, pitfalls. For a faster company, they're opportunities.

Paradox 1: Service versus Price

Remember the good old days, when consumers and business buyers expected service *or* price, but not both? Things were cheapest at the five-and-dime, but you knew you wouldn't get treated the way you did in a ritzy department store. If you wanted top quality or first-rate service, you knew you'd have to pay for it.

Today, of course, everyone wants both.

It isn't that market niches have disappeared. The motorist who buys a Mercedes knows she's getting a better car than if she'd bought a Chevrolet. And the guy who eats at McDonald's doesn't expect the quality he'd find at a fancy restaurant. But the consumer has raised the bar all over. That Chevrolet better be a great car for the money. That Chevrolet dealer better provide great warranty and repair service, or it's the last Chevrolet the customer will ever buy. And just because McDonald's is cheap doesn't mean the customer is willing to put up with greasy fries or slow service.

A lot of companies get hung up on this paradox. They don't know how to offer both first-rate service and a fair price. So they make compromises, and hope consumers won't notice. No doubt you have experienced this yourself. I don't know how many times you've stayed in hotels recently, but have you ever found one that offers you truly great service? I haven't—and I'm not even that demanding as a guest. All I want is my breakfast delivered on time, and faxes brought up to me when they come in, and someone to take my complaint seriously if the TV isn't working. Somehow, even expensive hotels don't seem to provide this level of service.

A faster company knows how to offer both world-class service and a competitive price.

We learned this skill at PSS over time. At first, we offered great service but we were on the expensive side. When our customers suddenly began worrying about how much things cost, we were at a disadvantage—unless we could change. So we did. We created mechanisms that let our customers save money, such as our Network Plus buying club. We introduced a low-priced private-label line of products. What we didn't do was compromise our commitment to same-day, no-hassle service. We just extended it to cover a broader variety of products.

To me, the lesson is clear: *You have to provide the service your customer wants and expects.* That comes first. If you can learn to do that, you can learn how to do it at an ever-lower cost—which means that you can reduce your prices and still maintain margins. Note that word *learn*. Nobody—and no company—is born knowing how to offer world-class service. But some learn. And once they do, they can meet their customers' expectations on price as well as on service.

Paradox 2: Continuous Improvement

I think the buzzword *continuous improvement* is just another way of saying *keeping people's heads in the game*.

If you want your company to get better year after year, there are plenty of methods available. There are the techniques of TQM and other business innovations. There's new technology. The real challenge is to keep your people fired up. If you have employees who want to improve, who care about bettering their performance, they'll find ways to do it.

That's a simple truth that's often missed. Companies introduce TQM or reengineer their business processes. They bring in new machines and new computer systems. The changes make a difference—for a while. Then the improvement levels out. And the reason is that people are just going about their business, doing what they're told, not really caring about what the next step might be.

At a faster company, everyone's head is in the game, all the time.

Partly, it's a matter of money. No doubt about it, money concentrates the mind. Unlimited commissions, fat bonuses, and generous stock-ownership plans give people a real stake in the business. They know it matters how well they do their jobs, and how their branches perform, and how all the other parts of the company perform. Their performance puts money in their pockets—and in their ESOP accounts, which build up real wealth over the long haul.

But it's also a matter of culture. A faster company such as PSS feels like a family. People want it to succeed because they want each other to succeed. And success *always* means bettering last year's performance.

How many companies close the books in December, look back on the past year, and figure that last year was pretty good so this year will probably be pretty good, too? That kind of attitude is a luxury you can't afford. You have to create an ethos that says: Forget what happened last month or last year. Focus on what you're doing right now—and on what you want to achieve this month or this year. You can always do better.

Paradox 3: Focus versus Growth

There's a recurring theme in business literature. Al Ries calls it *focus*. Tom Peters and Robert Waterman called it *sticking to the knitting*. Others use the term *core competencies*. Whatever the language, the meaning is the same. A company should do what it does best and not get involved in enterprises that require skills it doesn't have.

That's fine, and I believe it. And if your company is, say, Dell Computer, you can ride your industry's explosive growth and never have to worry about branching out or diversifying. But what do you do if you're in a mature industry? Or if you need to branch out just to maintain your growth rate and continue to create opportunities? How can you diversify without losing your focus? This is another pitfall for a lot of companies. They spot what looks like a great opportunity in an unrelated business and jump into it. In a year or two, they're figuring out how to cut their losses and get out.

The key here is to understand the difference between a *business* and a *business model*.

Your business is the industry you're in. It has its own practices and procedures. Every business is different. The fact that you're successful in book publishing doesn't mean you can run a pharmaceuticals company.

Your business model, in contrast, is *how* you do business. It's the kind of company you create, and how people in it work together, and what kind of value you bring to the customer. This book tells the story of PSS/World Medical, but it's about our business model more than our business. (If I wrote a book about how to run a medical-distribution company, how many people would buy it?)

So, the secret to diversification without losing focus is to enter a new business without losing your business model.

This is essentially what we've done with Diagnostic Imaging, our young division that provides sales and service of X-ray supplies and equipment. DI is not the same as PSS. It has a different set of customers, with different needs. As I explained earlier, same-day delivery of supplies is less important than fast response when an X-ray unit breaks down. If we tried to copy every PSS procedure at DI, we'd fail.

But the business model of DI is identical to PSS's. We define what constitutes real value to the customer. We set a standard that's higher than anyone else's—in this case, guaranteed response to a breakdown within two hours, any time of the day or night. We create systems to ensure that we can deliver what we say we'll deliver. We build a company that encourages people to have fun, that expects them to learn and grow, and that enables them to share in the wealth. DI has the same Top 20 as PSS. It's built around the same values.

So, you can clone your business model while moving into a new business. Note, of course, that we entered the X-ray industry rather than, say, the restaurant business. The closer you can stay to your core business, the more knowledgeable you'll be. In the future, you may see PSS divisions serving hospitals or nursing homes or dental offices. You probably won't see any PSS branches that say, "Eat Here."

Paradox 4: Loyalty

In times past, employees were supposed to be loyal to their companies and companies to their employees. The idea was, if you put in a good day's work for us year after year, we will keep you on, raise your pay, and give you a gold watch when you retire. That kind of blind loyalty, as we all know, vanished with yesterday's economy. The *value* of loyalty, however, hasn't changed. Every businessperson knows how important it is to have loyal employees and loyal customers. No company could last more than a week without at least some sense of reciprocal obligation between employer and employee.

So, how to cultivate loyalty, even in a turbulent marketplace?

You can't do it with words. I wish we could take all the high-falutin words that companies spout about how *We're All a Family Here* and *People Are Our Most Important Asset* and chuck 'em in the dump. The words are fine *if* you're walking the talk. If you aren't, they're worth nothing. They're worth less than nothing, really, since all they do is encourage cynicism.

Nor can you build loyalty with slippery concepts like "employability."

Some big companies these days are making a point of telling their employees that they can't guarantee them a job. What they can guarantee, they say, is employability. The companies will provide training. They'll help people acquire skills so they'll be able to find work if they're laid off or let go.

As you know, I'm not against training. I believe people should learn all the new skills they can. And if companies can help them, that's great. But what does it really say to employees when you tell them you'll guarantee employability? In my view, it says: *You're on your own, buster. You'll stay here as long as it's convenient for us and not one day longer. So you better have one eye on the job market all the time.*

At PSS, we have a different idea.

Sure, we know that nobody can guarantee a job for everybody all the time.

But when people have to be laid off through no fault of their own, that's a failure of management. The leaders of that organization have failed. We *never* want to fail in that way.

If we have to close a branch, for example—and we do have to, on occasion—we'll offer everybody a job somewhere else. If we acquire a company and can't keep everyone on board at that facility, we'll make sure they have first crack at opportunities elsewhere in the organization. If someone tries a new job and fails, we'll offer that person a soft landing. We're committed to grow partly so we can keep on offering these opportunities to people.

Then, too, the values on which our company is built are designed to encourage loyalty. Sharing the wealth, for example: All those bonuses and stock-ownership programs communicate the message, *We're all in this together.* That's a feeling that's missing from a lot of organizations. Our no-secrets open-book approach to management builds trust, which strengthens the loyalty.

You *can* build an organization based on mutual loyalty, even in today's economy. But you can't do it if you treat people as disposable. Sometimes, as a faster company, you will grow faster than you can handle, and you have blow-ups. PSS has had it happen twice, in 1991 and 1996. Yet no heads rolled. No one was fired. As a faster company, we recognize that we are in it together, as a team.

Why PSS Is Still in Its Infancy

PSS is like a lot of entrepreneurial companies in one respect: There's a certain glamor that attaches to the people who were there "way back when." We talk about how it used to be when we were just starting out. We tell the stories you've read in this book, like the "bomb" that wasn't a bomb. Because we're so open, word gets around about the six- or seven-figure portfolios of PSS stock that most of the early employees have accumulated. Like teenagers in a family, our newer employees will occasionally roll their eyes, because they've heard the stories once too often. But usually the reaction is different. It's, *Gee, I wish I'd been there at the start. I wish I'd been there when PSS was young.*

Whenever I hear this from one of the newer people, I say one thing: PSS *is* still young. It's in its infancy. And you're a part of it.

Think about it. Successful companies last for decades, even centuries. They build on their accomplishments. They enter new segments of their industries. The year this book is being published, 1998, is the year PSS turns 15 years old.

Procter & Gamble Corporation was 15 years old in 1852.

Ford Motor Company was 15 years old in 1918.

Heck, even Southwest Airlines, which most people think of as an upstart, turned 15 in 1983, the year PSS was founded.

In mentioning these great companies, I don't mean to put PSS in their class—yet. We're still a long ways from the Fortune 500, let alone from its top ranks. But that's just my point. Yes, we have grown like gangbusters. Not many companies reach a billion dollars in sales after only 15 years of operation. But we have a long, long road of opportunity stretching out ahead of us.

Look just at our own little business of delivering supplies to doctors' offices. It's a $5.5 billion business. We have less than 15 percent of the market.

The business of X-ray supplies and service is another $5 billion. We grew to challenge the number-one player in just our first year of operation. But we have huge possibilities for future growth here, as well.

Then there are all the segments of the health-care business that we haven't yet touched. Hospitals. Nursing homes. Dental offices. Even veterinarians' offices. They all need supplies. Of course, there are plenty of companies already in these niches. But there were plenty of companies serving physicians when we arrived, too. Our industry today is a playground of over $34 billion in sales.

And then there's the world.

It's funny: You don't often think of an American distribution company expanding overseas. It's one thing to export products. It's another thing to export a business model—or so you might think.

But we feel we can compete successfully virtually anywhere on the planet. Everybody has doctors and health-care institutions. Everybody needs supplies. And no country that we've uncovered has distributors who provide the level of service that we can provide. We learned when we took our first tentative steps into Europe, in 1997, that it will take a while for us to adapt to overseas markets. But we also learned that customers in Europe aren't so different from customers in the United States or anywhere else. If you give them better service than they have ever experienced, they just keep coming back. When we adopted the name PSS/World Medical, it was with the global marketplace in mind. There's no reason that we can't do in many, many countries exactly what we have learned to do in the United States.

One final word in closing:

There's a thrill involved in building a faster company. You create an organization of people who can accomplish great things. You see people challenge themselves, and learn, and grow. You build wealth and create opportunities, not just for yourself but for everyone involved in the business. We have had a thrilling ride at PSS—and the ride is only just beginning.

You, too, can experience this thrill. Get rid of the old, conventional ways of doing business! Learn to serve your customers in ways that competitors just can't copy. Build an organization that brings out the best in people and that rewards them according to their accomplishments. It's exciting, fun, and worthwhile. It helps make the world a better place. What more can you ask of any human endeavor?

EPILOGUE

What Really Matters

This book is about business. Business is great. I love it. Business gives customers the products and services they need. It creates wealth and provides opportunities. Building a company that can outstrip the competition—which means building a company that can do all those good things better than anyone else—is an accomplishment you and I and anyone else can be proud of.

But business isn't the whole of life. I was reminded of this one afternoon about five years ago.

I was in Omaha, Nebraska, on a business trip, and I happened to have an afternoon off. I figured I would drive out and see the famous Boys Town home located just outside Omaha. When I got there, I saw they had a banner up, celebrating Boys Town's seventieth anniversary.

Driving around the place, I was amazed. It was so big! Later, I learned that Boys Town serves more than 6,000 children. Talking with people there, I understood how the organization could serve so many people. They own large amounts of real estate in the Omaha area. They have an endowment of hundreds of millions of dollars. Thanks to the old movie starring Spencer Tracy and Mickey Rooney, people all over the United States have made millions of dollars' worth of contributions and bequests to Boys Town. They continue to do so even now.

Seeing Boys Town, I thought of the Virginia Home for Boys, where I had grown up.

At that point, I hadn't had much contact with the Home. Sure, I gave it a modest contribution every year. But it wasn't much. And I didn't really know a lot about what was going on there.

I decided to change that.

When I got back home, I called the director of the Home. I asked him to tell me how many boys were living there, and where they came from. I asked him about the Home's endowment, and what services they were able to offer. Then I asked how old the Home was. His answers blew me away. The Home was approaching 150 years old, and yet our endowment was about equal to the monthly interest on the Boys Town endowment. There were many fewer boys there than when I lived at the Home, and much of the Home's support came from the state. Because they were supported by the state, many boys cycled in and out of the Home. They'd live there until the state found a foster family to place them with, which, of course, was cheaper. Then when the foster family didn't work out, they'd wind up back at the Home. Of course, some boys never made it back. They'd wind up in prison, or on the streets, or dead.

I decided to try to make a difference. Since that time, I have worked with my brother, Jimmy, and with Jim Carr, Kevin Wood, and so many more who also grew up in the Home. We want the Home to become less dependent on state funding, and to offer boys the kind of stable environment that made such a difference to us.

We have set up a foundation, which is raising money for the Home. My personal goal is to leave a minimum of $100 million to serve the Virginia Home for Boys and other children's homes in America.

Today, we guarantee every boy from the Home who graduates from high school a four-year college education, at no cost to him. Our first graduates went to college five years ago.

We have begun to organize other alumni to support the Home. One of the alumni, for example, John Salgado, runs a small construction company. He is always there, fixing things up, cutting the grass, and doing odd jobs. John Salgado is one of my real heroes in life and is a role model for every boy from the Virginia Home for Boys.

I have been privileged to have many boys from the Home visit me in Jacksonville. We'll go out to a ball game or a movie. We'll spend time together, just talking. I learn a lot from them, and maybe they learn something from me. At the very least, they see that a childhood spent in the Virginia Home for Boys isn't a handicap. It doesn't mean you can't be successful. It doesn't mean you can't make something of your life. In fact, one of the most exciting events in my life was winning the Horatio Alger Award in 1997. The Horatio Alger Association of Distinguished Americans gives away more college scholarships than any organization in America, and their award—a "rags-to-riches" recognition—meant the world to me. But it will mean even more to the Home, because it's a tangible symbol that a boy who grows up there can accomplish just about anything he sets his mind to.

You, the reader, have already done a little bit for the Home without knowing it: All of my earnings from the sale of this book will go straight to the Boys Home Foundation. But I'd like you to think for a moment not just about the Boys Home, but about all the organizations and people in this world who need help. There are a lot of them. They shouldn't have to depend on the government for resources. (And the government doesn't do a great job of supporting them anyway.)

I know: You can't solve all the problems. But it doesn't matter. Start with a few, or just one. Do something. If you get involved in your own community, you'll quickly find out what needs to be done. And you'll learn something even more important: *that you can make a difference.*

P.S. **A Money-Back Guarantee (sort of):** If you find you can't use a single idea from this book, please send me an e-mail at pkelly@pssd.com or write me at PSS, 4345 Southpoint Blvd., Jacksonville FL 32216 USA. I'll donate one share of PSSI to the Boys Home Foundation in your name.

INDEX